DETRIMENTAL KINDNESS

HOW NOT TO LOSE YOURSELF WHILE HELPING OTHERS

JASON JOHNSON

1st edition, July 2025
ISBN-13: 979-8-218-72471-9
Printed in the United States of America

DEDICATION

To the ones who gave until they were empty.

Who stayed quiet to keep the peace.

Who confused self-abandonment with love.

This book is for you.

May it remind you that kindness isn't real if it costs you yourself.

And that your voice, your needs, your boundaries

are not just valid, they are vital.

CONTENTS

INTRODUCTION

THE KINDNESS THAT'S KILLING YOU

I was lying on my back, staring at the ceiling at 2 AM, my body aching from six hours of moving furniture that wasn't mine. My phone buzzed. A text from the friend whose apartment I'd just helped relocate: "Thanks man."

That was it. No lunch. No real gratitude. Just two words after I'd sacrificed my entire weekend, again.

But here's the thing that kept me awake that night: it wasn't his lack of appreciation that bothered me. It was the realization that I'd said yes before he'd even finished asking. That I'd canceled my own plans without a second thought. That I'd spent the entire day silently resenting him while wearing a smile.

I was performing kindness, and it was slowly killing me.

Maybe you know this feeling. The exhaustion that comes not from doing too much, but from being too much for everyone else. The quiet resentment that builds when you give and give, yet somehow feel invisible. The confusion of being praised as "the good one," "the reliable one," "the helper," while feeling completely empty inside.

If you've ever wondered why being kind feels so hard, why your generosity seems to attract takers, or why you feel guilty every time you try to put yourself first, this book is for you.

The Problem Hiding in Plain Sight

We live in a world that celebrates selflessness. Social media is full of quotes about giving more, doing more, being more. We're told that good people sacrifice, that love means putting others first, that kindness requires self-denial.

But what happens when kindness becomes a performance you can't escape? When being "good" costs you your peace, your energy, and eventually, your sense of self?

I spent years as a fitness coach watching people transform their bodies while their emotional lives remained stuck in patterns of over-giving and under-receiving. Clients would get physically stronger while becoming emotionally depleted. They'd master their nutrition while neglecting their need for rest. They'd achieve their fitness goals while losing themselves in relationships that demanded constant accommodation.

That's when I realized something profound: the same patterns that keep people stuck in unhealthy relationships with food often show up in their relationships with others. The inability to say no. The guilt around self-care. The belief that their needs don't matter as much as everyone else's.

The Moment Everything Changed

My awakening didn't come from a dramatic crisis. It came from that quiet moment in my car after helping someone move, looking at myself in the rearview mirror and asking, "What the hell am I doing?"

I realized I'd become addicted to being needed. I said yes to every request, picked up every call, solved every problem, not because I wanted to, but because I was terrified of what would happen if I didn't. I'd confused being useful with being loved.

But the most painful realization was this: the very kindness I thought made me valuable was actually making me invisible. People saw what I could do for them, not who I was. And I'd trained them to relate to me that way.

That night, I made a decision that changed everything. I decided to figure out why good people like me (like you) end up feeling so empty despite giving everything we have.

What I Discovered

Through my own journey and years of working with clients caught in similar patterns, I've identified something I call **"Detrimental Kindness"** – kindness that hurts the giver more than it helps the receiver.

It's the yes that's really a no. The smile that masks exhaustion. The helpfulness that becomes a trap. The love that requires you to disappear.

Detrimental kindness looks generous from the outside, but it feels like slow suffocation on the inside. It's what happens when our desire to be good becomes disconnected from our need to be whole.

Here's what I learned that no one talks about: **most of what we call kindness isn't actually kind.** It's fear wearing a helpful mask. It's the need for approval disguised as generosity. It's self-abandonment marketed as virtue.

Real kindness (the kind that actually heals and connects) includes the giver. It doesn't ask you to bleed so others can feel better. It doesn't demand that you silence your truth to avoid conflict. And it certainly doesn't require you to disappear to prove your love.

Why This Matters Now

We're living through an epidemic of "good people" feeling terrible. Seventy-six percent of people report feeling emotionally drained from trying to meet others' expectations. Depression and anxiety rates are climbing among the most caring, most helpful, most "together" people you know.

Meanwhile, we're told the solution is self-care, as if the problem is simply that we need better boundaries or more bubble baths. But detrimental kindness isn't solved by adding more to your routine. It's solved by questioning the beliefs that created the pattern in the first place.

The cost of continuing this way isn't just personal exhaustion. When good people burn out from giving, the world loses their authentic contribution. When kind people retreat because their kindness has been weaponized against them, we all suffer.

But when people learn to be kind in a way that honors their own humanity, that's when real healing happens. Not just for them, but for everyone in their orbit.

What You'll Find in This Book

This isn't another book about boundaries or self-care, though both matter. This is about fundamentally redefining what it means to be kind. It's about learning to give from fullness instead of emptiness.

It's about discovering that the most generous thing you can do is show up as your whole self.

We'll move through three essential phases:

RECOGNIZE: You'll learn to identify the subtle ways detrimental kindness shows up in your life. You'll understand the difference between giving from love and giving from fear. And you'll discover why your body has been trying to warn you about these patterns all along.

RELEASE: You'll learn to let go of the guilt that keeps you trapped, the beliefs that keep you small, and the identity that requires your constant sacrifice. This isn't about becoming selfish. It's about becoming honest.

RECLAIM: You'll discover what authentic kindness actually looks like. You'll learn to set boundaries that honor both your care for others and your care for yourself. And you'll create a life where your kindness flows from choice, not compulsion.

Who This Book Is For

This book is for the over-giver, the people-pleaser, the one everyone counts on. It's for the person who can't rest without guilt, who fears disappointing others more than disappointing themselves.

It's for the helper who's forgotten they need help too. The giver who's lost touch with their ability to receive. The kind person who's tired of being taken for granted.

It's for anyone who's ever felt like they're performing their way through life, hoping that if they just give enough, do enough, be enough, they'll finally earn the love and acceptance they crave.

If you've been waiting for permission to matter in your own life, consider this your invitation.

Who This Book Is Not For

If you believe that boundaries are selfish, this book will challenge you. If you think that good people should never disappoint anyone, this will be uncomfortable. If your identity depends on being the hero in everyone else's story, this book will ask you to consider a different way.

This isn't about becoming less caring. It's about caring more consciously. It's not about loving others less. It's about including yourself in the category of people worth loving.

A Promise and a Warning

I promise you this: the kindness you'll discover in these pages will be more authentic, more sustainable, and more healing than anything you've practiced before. You'll learn to give without depleting yourself, to love without losing yourself, and to help others without abandoning your own needs.

But I also need to warn you: this journey will disrupt some relationships. People who are used to your unlimited availability may not appreciate your newfound boundaries. Those who benefited from your self-sacrifice may resist your transformation.

Some connections will deepen as you show up more authentically. Others may fade as you stop enabling unhealthy dynamics. This isn't failure. It's clarification. You'll discover who was there for you versus who was there for what you could provide.

The Freedom Waiting for You

What lies ahead isn't a life without challenges, but a life grounded in truth. You'll still care deeply (perhaps more deeply than ever), but you'll care consciously. You'll still help others, but you'll help from a place of choice rather than compulsion.

You'll discover that the world doesn't need your depletion. It needs your authentic presence. And that presence, rooted in kindness that includes you, is the greatest gift you can offer.

The journey back to yourself begins now. It starts with the radical recognition that kindness isn't real if it costs you yourself.

Let's begin.

CHAPTER 1

WHEN KINDNESS COSTS TOO MUCH

There's a moment that comes to everyone who gives too much. It's quiet but unmistakable. You're standing in your kitchen, or sitting in your car, or lying in bed at night, and suddenly you realize: you don't recognize your own life anymore.

Everything looks right from the outside. You're helpful, reliable, loved by many. But inside, you feel like you're slowly disappearing. You've become so good at being what everyone else needs that you've forgotten who you actually are.

That moment came for me on a Tuesday evening. I'd just finished helping a colleague with a project that had somehow become my responsibility, despite having nothing to do with my actual job.

As I finally sat down to eat dinner at 9 PM, I looked around my apartment and felt like a stranger in my own space.

When had I stopped having time for myself? When had "helping" become the only way I knew how to relate to people? When had kindness become this heavy thing I carried instead of this natural expression of who I was?

If you've ever felt this way, you're not alone. And you're not crazy. You've just been practicing a form of kindness that was never meant to be sustainable.

The Kindness That Doesn't Feel Kind

We need to talk about something most people won't say out loud: sometimes our kindness feels terrible. Not because we don't want to help, but because somewhere along the way, kindness stopped being a choice and became a compulsion.

You say yes before you've even considered if you want to. You smile through conversations that drain you. You offer help you don't have the energy to give. You accommodate everyone else's schedule while yours falls apart.

This isn't the kindness you set out to practice. This is kindness that's been hijacked by fear, guilt, and the desperate need to be accepted.

I remember talking to Sarah, a client who came to me exhausted from managing her entire family's emotional needs. "I love them," she said, tears in her eyes, "but I feel like I'm drowning. Every conversation is about their problems. Every holiday is planned around their preferences. I can't remember the last time someone asked how I was doing and actually waited for an answer."

Sarah wasn't unkind. She was practicing what I call "costly kindness" – generosity that demands everything from the giver while expecting nothing in return.

The Three Faces of Costly Kindness

Through my work with people caught in these patterns, I've noticed that costly kindness typically shows up in three distinct ways:

The Automatic Yes This is when your mouth says yes before your brain has time to process the request. Someone asks for a favor, and you're already nodding. A colleague needs help, and you're volunteering before they finish explaining. Your family wants something, and you're rearranging your life to accommodate them.

The automatic yes feels like being kind, but it's actually a nervous system response. You've been conditioned to believe that saying no is dangerous, so your body responds to requests like emergency situations that require immediate compliance.

The Guilt Response

This happens when you feel responsible for everyone else's emotional state. When someone is disappointed, you feel like you failed them. When there's conflict, you immediately start thinking about how to fix it. When someone is struggling, you assume it's your job to rescue them.

The guilt response makes you feel noble and necessary, but it's exhausting. You end up carrying emotional weight that was never yours to begin with.

The Performance Trap This is when you curate your personality to match what others seem to want. You're agreeable in meetings even when you disagree. You laugh at jokes that aren't funny. You pretend to be fine when you're falling apart. You become whoever you think people need you to be.

The performance trap makes you feel safe and liked, but it slowly erases your authentic self. You become so good at being agreeable that you forget what you actually think and feel.

Why Good People Get Trapped

Here's what I've learned that might surprise you: the people most likely to get caught in costly kindness are often the most emotionally intelligent, empathetic, and genuinely caring people you'll meet. This isn't a character flaw. It's a feature that's been exploited.

When you're naturally attuned to others' needs, it's easy to start prioritizing those needs over your own. When you're good at reading a room, you automatically adjust yourself to keep everyone comfortable. When you genuinely care about people, the thought of disappointing them feels unbearable.

But here's the trap: the more you accommodate, the more people expect accommodation. The more you say yes, the harder it becomes to say no. The more you put yourself last, the more invisible your own needs become.

Mark, another client, described it perfectly: "I became so good at being what everyone needed that I forgot I was allowed to need things too. I thought being low-maintenance was a virtue, but really I was just slowly disappearing."

The Hidden Costs Nobody Talks About

We talk a lot about the benefits of kindness – how it makes us happier, healthier, more connected. But we rarely discuss what happens when kindness becomes compulsive rather than conscious.

Your Energy Becomes Currency When you're always available, always helping, always accommodating, your energy becomes something people expect to access whenever they need it. You become an emotional ATM that everyone assumes is always full, even when you're running on fumes.

Your Preferences Become Irrelevant When you're always flexible, always willing to go along with others' plans, people stop asking what you want. They assume you're fine with whatever they decide. Eventually, you might stop knowing what you want too.

Your Problems Become Invisible When you're always the helper, always the strong one, always the one who has it together, people stop checking on you. They assume you're fine. They take your stability for granted. Your struggles become invisible because you've trained everyone to see you as unbreakable.

Your Voice Becomes Optional When you avoid conflict, when you go along to get along, when you keep your opinions to yourself to maintain harmony, your voice gradually gets quieter. People stop asking what you think because they've learned you'll agree with whatever they say anyway.

The Moment of Recognition

The turning point for most people comes when they realize they've been living for everyone else's approval while completely neglecting their own needs. It's the moment when you understand that your kindness has become a prison, not a gift.

For me, that moment came when I realized I was resentful toward the very people I was trying to help. I was angry at them for asking too much, but I'd never told them where my limits were. I was frustrated that they didn't appreciate my sacrifices, but I'd never explained what those sacrifices cost me.

That's when I understood something crucial: **resentment is often a sign that we've been giving beyond our capacity for too long.**

It wasn't their fault for taking what I offered. It was my responsibility for offering more than I could sustainably give.

The Body's Warning System

Your body has been trying to tell you something about costly kindness, but you might have learned to ignore its signals. Physical exhaustion that sleep doesn't fix. Tension headaches after difficult conversations. Stomach knots when your phone rings. A racing heart when someone asks for help.

These aren't signs of weakness. They're signs of wisdom. Your nervous system understands what your mind might be reluctant to admit: something about this pattern isn't working.

Lisa, a nurse I worked with, described it this way: "My body was keeping score even when my mind was trying to convince me everything was fine. I was getting sick more often, sleeping poorly, and feeling anxious all the time. My body knew I was overextended before my brain was willing to admit it."

The Difference Between Kind and Costly

Real kindness flows from a place of fullness, not emptiness. It comes from choice, not compulsion. It enhances relationships rather than creating resentment. It includes the giver in the equation.

Costly kindness, on the other hand, depletes the giver while creating dependency in the receiver. It comes from fear of rejection rather than genuine care. It maintains unhealthy dynamics rather than fostering growth.

The difference isn't in the action itself – both might involve helping someone or saying yes to a request. The difference is in the internal state of the giver and the sustainability of the pattern.

When kindness costs too much, it stops being kind to anyone involved.

What Changes When You Recognize the Cost

Recognizing that your kindness has become costly isn't about becoming less caring. It's about becoming more conscious about how you care. It's about understanding that sustainable kindness requires you to include yourself in the equation.

When you start paying attention to the cost of your giving, several things shift:

You begin to notice the difference between requests that energize you and those that drain you. You start paying attention to your internal response to people's needs rather than automatically saying yes. You become aware of the stories you tell yourself about what makes you a good person.

Most importantly, you start to understand that taking care of yourself isn't selfish – it's necessary. You can't give what you don't have. You can't sustain what depletes you. And you can't love others authentically if you don't love yourself enough to honor your own limits.

The Permission You've Been Waiting For

If you've been practicing costly kindness, you might need to hear this: **You are allowed to cost something too.** Your time, your energy, your emotional bandwidth – these things have value. You're allowed to protect them. You're allowed to be selective about how you share them.

This doesn't make you selfish. It makes you sustainable.

The world doesn't need your depletion. It needs your authentic presence. And authentic presence is only possible when you're caring for yourself with the same tenderness you show others.

Tomorrow, we'll explore how to recognize the specific ways costly kindness shows up in daily life. But for now, just notice. Notice where kindness feels heavy instead of light. Notice where giving feels compulsive instead of chosen. Notice where you might be paying a price you never agreed to pay.

The first step toward sustainable kindness is honest recognition of what the current pattern is costing you. And that recognition, however uncomfortable, is actually the beginning of your return to authentic generosity.

You deserve kindness too. Starting with the kindness you show yourself.

CHAPTER 2

THE THREE FACES OF DETRIMENTAL KINDNESS

I used to think there was only one way to be too kind: saying yes too much. But after working with dozens of clients and examining my own patterns, I've discovered that detrimental kindness is far more sophisticated than simple over-accommodation. It's a shape-shifter that adapts to your personality, your circumstances, and your deepest fears about being rejected or abandoned.

Understanding these different expressions is crucial because you can't change what you can't see clearly. And detrimental kindness is masterful at disguising itself as virtue, making it nearly impossible to recognize until you know what to look for.

Let me introduce you to what I call the Three Faces of Detrimental Kindness. Most people recognize themselves in at least one of these patterns, and many cycle between all three depending on the situation. Each face represents a different survival strategy, but all three share the same devastating outcome: they slowly erode your sense of self while creating the very rejection and disconnection they were designed to prevent.

Face One: The Accommodator

The Accommodator believes that flexibility equals love. If someone needs something changed, moved, rescheduled, or adjusted, the Accommodator immediately rearranges their life to make it happen. They're the ones who say, "Whatever works for you works for me," even when it doesn't work for them at all.

I lived as an Accommodator for years without realizing it. I thought I was being easygoing and considerate. In reality, I was so afraid of being seen as difficult that I'd become a human pretzel, twisting myself into whatever shape others needed.

The Accommodator's signature phrase is "I'm flexible." But here's what I learned: when you're always flexible, you teach people that your preferences don't matter. You train them to make decisions without considering your needs because you've shown them that you'll adapt no matter what.

How the Accommodator Thinks The Accommodator's internal dialogue sounds reasonable, even noble:

- "I don't want to be difficult"
- "Their needs seem more important than mine"
- "I can handle it, so I should"
- "It's easier if I just go along"
- "I don't want to cause problems"

This thinking pattern creates what I call "preference paralysis" – the gradual loss of connection to your own wants and needs. When you've spent years prioritizing others' preferences, your own desires can feel foreign, selfish, or simply unclear.

Rachel's Story Rachel came to me after realizing she hadn't made a single decision about her own life in over two years. Every choice, from where to eat dinner to which vacation to take, had been determined by someone else's preferences.

"I thought I was being considerate," she told me. "But I realized I was actually afraid. Afraid that if I expressed a preference and someone disagreed, they'd think I was selfish or demanding. So I just... disappeared. I became whoever they needed me to be."

The breaking point came when her husband asked what she wanted for her birthday. She couldn't answer. She'd become so practiced at accommodating others that she'd lost touch with her own desires. "I sat there for ten minutes trying to think of something I wanted," she recalled. "And I realized I didn't even know who I was anymore without someone else's preferences to follow."

Rachel's accommodating started in childhood with divorced parents who put her in the middle of their conflicts. She learned that being agreeable meant being safe, that having strong preferences caused tension, and that love came through making other people's lives easier. By adulthood, accommodation had become so automatic that she did it without conscious thought.

The Hidden Cost of Accommodation Accommodators often pride themselves on being low-maintenance, but this comes at a steep price. When you consistently prioritize others' preferences over your own, several things happen:

You lose touch with what you actually want. Your decision-making muscles atrophy from lack of use. People begin to see you as agreeable rather than interesting. You start to feel invisible in your own life.

Most painfully, you begin to resent the very people you're trying to please. Not because they're demanding, but because you've taught them that your needs are negotiable while theirs are not.

The Accommodator also tends to attract decision-makers who are comfortable being accommodated. Over time, this creates relationships where one person does all the choosing while the other does all the adapting. The irony is that this dynamic often leads to the very rejection the Accommodator fears, as people lose respect for someone who never advocates for themselves.

The Daily Life of an Accommodator Accommodation shows up in countless small moments:

- Always letting others choose the restaurant, then eating food you don't particularly enjoy
- Agreeing to weekend plans that exhaust you rather than suggesting alternatives
- Taking on extra work because "someone has to do it" and you're available
- Staying quiet in meetings when you disagree with the direction
- Adjusting your schedule repeatedly to accommodate others' changing needs
- Saying "I don't care" when you actually do care, but feel like your opinion doesn't matter

Each individual accommodation might seem minor, but collectively they create a life that feels borrowed rather than owned.

Face Two: The Rescuer

The Rescuer believes that love means solving other people's problems. They're the ones who jump in to fix, save, and manage everyone else's emotional crises. They can't see someone struggling without immediately offering solutions, support, or intervention.

Rescuers are often praised for their helpfulness, which reinforces the pattern. They become known as the person everyone calls when life gets difficult. And while this feels meaningful, it's actually a trap that keeps both the Rescuer and the people they help stuck in unhealthy dynamics.

The Rescuer's Internal World The Rescuer's thoughts are driven by a combination of genuine care and hidden fears:

- "They need me"
- "I'm the only one who can help them"
- "If I don't help, something terrible will happen"
- "Their problems are my responsibility"
- "I should be strong enough to handle this"

What the Rescuer doesn't often acknowledge is the secondary gain they receive from being needed. Rescuing provides a sense of purpose, importance, and control. It feels better to focus on others' fixable problems than to face your own complex emotions and needs.

David's Awakening David was the family problem-solver. When his sister struggled with money, he paid her bills. When his brother faced relationship issues, David became the mediator. When his parents had conflicts, he served as the go-between.

"I felt important," he admitted. "Like I was the glue holding everyone together. But I also felt exhausted. Every phone call was a crisis. Every family gathering was about someone's drama.

I realized I wasn't helping them grow stronger. I was helping them stay dependent."

David's rescuing pattern began when his father left the family when David was twelve. His mother fell into depression, and David stepped up to take care of everyone – his younger siblings, the household responsibilities, and his mother's emotional needs. Being the rescuer became his identity, his value, and his way of ensuring his family stayed together.

The moment that changed everything was when David went through his own difficult period – a job loss that left him financially and emotionally drained. When he reached out to his family for support, they were either unavailable or uncomfortable with the role reversal. He'd trained them to see him as the helper, not as someone who might need help.

"I realized I'd created relationships where I was only valued for what I could provide," David said. "When I needed them to show up for me, they didn't know how. I'd never taught them that I had needs too."

The Rescuer's Dilemma Rescuers often struggle with what psychologists call "helper's high" – the addictive feeling of being needed. This creates a paradox: the more they help, the more help is required. They inadvertently enable the very problems they're trying to solve.

The pattern works like this: someone has a problem, the Rescuer solves it, the person feels grateful (temporarily), and the Rescuer feels valuable. But because the person hasn't developed their own problem-solving skills, the issues recur, often in more complex forms.

Rescuers also tend to attract people who benefit from being rescued. Over time, their relationships become functionally imbalanced, with the Rescuer always giving and others always taking. This creates what I call "learned helplessness in reverse" – the Rescuer becomes so good at solving problems that others stop trying to solve their own.

The Many Forms of Rescuing Rescuing doesn't always look dramatic. It often shows up in subtle, everyday ways:

- Giving unsolicited advice when someone shares a problem
- Taking on tasks that others are capable of doing themselves
- Making excuses for other people's behavior or poor choices
- Lending money repeatedly to the same financially irresponsible person
- Doing emotional labor that others should be doing for themselves
- Staying up late helping with projects that aren't your responsibility
- Intervening in conflicts that don't involve you

Each rescue mission reinforces the belief that you're responsible for others' wellbeing and that your worth comes from your ability to solve problems.

Face Three: The Peacekeeper

The Peacekeeper believes that harmony equals safety. They'll do almost anything to avoid conflict, disagreement, or tension. They're the ones who change the subject when conversations get uncomfortable, who agree publicly while disagreeing privately, who absorb others' anger rather than risk a confrontation.

Peacekeepers often come from families where conflict was scary, unpredictable, or emotionally dangerous. They learned early that keeping everyone calm was their job, and they became incredibly skilled at reading emotional temperatures and adjusting accordingly.

The Peacekeeper's Mental Gymnastics The Peacekeeper's thoughts are focused on maintaining stability at any cost:

- "It's not worth fighting about"
- "I'll just agree to keep the peace"
- "Someone needs to be the mature one here"
- "Conflict always makes things worse"
- "If I stay quiet, this will blow over"

What Peacekeepers don't realize is that their conflict avoidance often creates the very instability they're trying to prevent. Issues that aren't addressed don't disappear – they grow larger and more problematic over time.

Maria's Revelation Maria grew up in a household where her parents' fights were explosive and frightening. She learned to become a tiny emotional barometer, constantly monitoring the mood and doing whatever it took to keep things peaceful.

As an adult, this translated into being unable to express disagreement with anyone about anything. At work, she agreed with ideas she thought were terrible. In friendships, she went along with plans that didn't interest her. In her marriage, she avoided bringing up issues that needed to be addressed.

"I thought I was being mature and diplomatic," she said. "But I was actually being dishonest. I was prioritizing temporary peace over authentic relationship. And the peace wasn't even real – it was just me swallowing my truth to avoid discomfort."

The turning point came when Maria realized that her avoidance of conflict was actually creating more problems. Issues she wouldn't address grew larger. Resentment built up in silence. Her relationships felt surface-level because she never shared what she really thought or felt.

"My marriage almost ended because I'd been agreeing with everything for so long that my husband didn't know who I really was,"

Maria explained. "When I finally started expressing my actual opinions, he said it felt like he was meeting me for the first time. We had to rebuild our relationship from the ground up."

The Peacekeeper's Paradox Peacekeepers often believe they're maintaining harmony, but they're actually preventing authentic connection. Real intimacy requires the ability to disagree, to work through differences, to have difficult conversations. When you avoid all conflict, you also avoid the deeper understanding that comes from navigating disagreement together.

Peacekeepers also tend to attract people who are comfortable with one-sided relationships. Because they don't push back, don't challenge, don't create any friction, they can end up surrounded by people who expect constant agreement and accommodation.

The Subtle Ways Peacekeeping Shows Up Peacekeeping manifests in both obvious and hidden ways:

- Changing the subject when conversations become tense
- Laughing off insults or dismissive comments instead of addressing them
- Agreeing with opinions you find offensive to avoid argument
- Taking blame for things that aren't your fault to end disagreements
- Making jokes to diffuse tension rather than addressing the underlying issue

- Staying silent when you witness unfairness or mistreatment
- Apologizing excessively, even when you've done nothing wrong

Each act of peacekeeping reinforces the belief that your authentic thoughts and feelings are dangerous and that relationships can't handle honest disagreement.

How the Faces Interact and Evolve

Most people don't fit neatly into just one category. You might be an Accommodator at work, a Rescuer in your family, and a Peacekeeper in your romantic relationship. Or you might cycle through all three faces depending on your stress level, the relationship dynamic, or what's at stake.

I've also noticed that people often "graduate" from one face to another as their lives change. A Peacekeeper might become an Accommodator when they enter a new relationship. An Accommodator might become a Rescuer when they have children. A Rescuer might become a Peacekeeper when their rescuing efforts repeatedly fail.

The Stress Factor When stress levels increase, people often default to their primary detrimental kindness pattern more intensely. The Accommodator becomes even more flexible, the Rescuer takes on even more problems, and the Peacekeeper avoids conflict even more desperately. This is why these patterns can feel so entrenched during difficult periods – they're actually coping mechanisms that feel necessary for survival.

The Relationship Dynamic Effect Different relationships can trigger different faces. You might be a strong boundary-setter with your colleagues but a complete Accommodator with your parents. You might rescue your adult children while keeping perfect peace with your spouse. Understanding that these patterns are contextual, not fixed personality traits, is crucial for change.

The common thread connecting all three faces is fear: fear of rejection, abandonment, conflict, or being seen as selfish. Each face represents a different strategy for staying safe and connected, but all three ultimately create the opposite of what they're trying to achieve.

The Underlying Beliefs That Drive All Three Faces

Regardless of which face you most identify with, detrimental kindness is typically powered by similar core beliefs:

- My worth depends on my usefulness to others
- Other people's needs are more important than mine
- Conflict is dangerous and should be avoided at all costs
- If I'm not constantly giving, people will leave
- Good people don't have limits or boundaries

- Love must be earned through self-sacrifice
- My feelings and opinions don't matter as much as others'
- I am responsible for everyone else's emotional state
- Being needed is the same as being loved

These beliefs feel true, especially if they were formed early in life during times when they actually were protective. But they're learned responses that can be examined, questioned, and ultimately changed.

Recognition Without Judgment

If you've recognized yourself in any of these faces, the first impulse might be to judge yourself harshly. You might think, "I'm so weak," or "I should have known better," or "I'm such a pushover."

But here's what I want you to understand: these patterns developed for good reasons. They were survival strategies that helped you navigate challenging situations, maintain relationships, and feel safe in an uncertain world. They served a purpose.

The problem isn't that you developed these patterns. The problem is that they may no longer be serving you. What helped you survive in one context might be limiting you in another.

Sarah's Integration Sarah, who identified strongly as an Accommodator, had a breakthrough when she reframed her pattern this way: "I developed incredible flexibility because I grew up in chaos. Being adaptable was a superpower that helped me thrive in an unpredictable environment. But now I'm in a stable relationship with a patient partner, and I don't need that level of flexibility anymore. I can use that skill consciously rather than automatically."

This shift from judgment to understanding opened up space for conscious choice. Sarah could appreciate the wisdom of her adaptation while also recognizing that it was time to evolve.

She began what she called "conscious accommodation" – choosing when to be flexible based on the situation and her capacity, rather than automatically bending to every request. "I still accommodate sometimes," she explained, "but now it's a choice I make from strength, not a compulsion I follow from fear."

The Beginning of Change

Recognizing which face (or faces) of detrimental kindness you've been wearing is the first step toward transformation. But recognition alone isn't enough. The goal isn't to completely eliminate these tendencies – they're part of your caring nature and can be valuable when used consciously.

The goal is to move from unconscious reaction to conscious choice. To ask yourself: "Am I accommodating because it serves the situation, or because I'm afraid of conflict? Am I helping because I have something valuable to offer, or because I need to feel needed?

Am I keeping peace because it's genuinely appropriate, or because I'm avoiding necessary conversations?"

These questions aren't meant to create more self-criticism. They're meant to create awareness – the foundation of all lasting change. When you can see your patterns clearly, without judgment, you can begin to choose differently.

In the next chapter, we'll explore how these patterns show up in your body and emotions – the warning signs that you're operating from detrimental kindness rather than authentic generosity. Because your body often knows what your mind is reluctant to admit: when kindness stops serving and starts depleting.

Understanding these signals is crucial for developing what I call "conscious kindness" – generosity that enhances rather than diminishes both the giver and receiver. But first, you need to learn to listen to the wisdom your body has been trying to share all along.

CHAPTER 3

THE HIDDEN COST OF OVERGIVING

You can hide exhaustion behind a smile. You can mask resentment with helpfulness. You can disguise depletion as dedication. But you can't hide from your body forever.

Your body has been keeping score of every forced yes, every swallowed need, every moment you chose others' comfort over your own truth. While your mind might rationalize and minimize, your body accumulates the evidence of overgiving like a careful accountant tracking debts that never get paid.

I learned this the hard way during what I now call my "breakdown period" – three months when my body essentially went on strike. Chronic headaches, constant fatigue, digestive issues that no doctor could explain, and an immune system so compromised that I caught every bug that went around. My mind kept insisting I was fine, that I just needed to push through, but my body was staging a full rebellion.

The wake-up call came when I found myself crying in the grocery store checkout line for no apparent reason. Not sad crying – just an overwhelming flood of emotion that seemed to come from nowhere. That's when I realized that all the costs I'd been ignoring had finally compounded beyond my ability to manage them.

The hidden costs of overgiving aren't just emotional or relational. They're physical, psychological, and spiritual. They affect every aspect of your life, often in ways so gradual that you don't notice until the damage is significant.

The Physical Toll: When Your Body Rebels

Your nervous system doesn't distinguish between a physical threat and the emotional threat of disappointing someone. When you're constantly saying yes despite your internal no, when you're perpetually accommodating others while neglecting yourself, your body responds as if you're under constant attack.

The Stress Response Cycle Every time you override your authentic response to please someone else, your body activates its stress response system. Your heart rate increases, stress hormones flood your system, and your muscles tense in preparation for action. But because you're not actually fighting or fleeing – you're just smiling and saying yes – that stress energy has nowhere to go. It gets trapped in your body, accumulating like sediment in a river.

Over time, this chronic activation leads to what I call "stress residue" – a constant low-level state of physical tension that becomes so familiar you might not even notice it anymore. You might think it's normal to have tight shoulders, frequent headaches, or digestive issues. But these are often your body's way of expressing what your voice won't: that something isn't right.

Lisa's Physical Awakening Lisa, a social worker and mother of three, came to me after her doctor couldn't find a medical reason for her chronic fatigue and frequent illnesses. She was getting sick every month, sleeping poorly, and experiencing what she called "bone-deep exhaustion" that rest couldn't cure.

"I thought I was just getting older," she told me. "But when we started tracking my symptoms alongside my overgiving episodes, a clear pattern emerged. I'd get sick right after family visits where I'd taken care of everyone. I'd have digestive problems after weeks of saying yes to extra projects at work. My body was basically screaming at me to slow down, but I kept interpreting the signals as personal weakness."

Once Lisa began honoring her body's signals and reducing her overgiving, her physical symptoms dramatically improved. "I realized my body wasn't betraying me," she said. "It was trying to protect me. I just wasn't listening."

Common Physical Manifestations The physical costs of overgiving show up differently for different people, but some patterns are remarkably consistent:

Chronic fatigue that sleep doesn't resolve, because emotional exhaustion is as depleting as physical exertion. Tension headaches and jaw pain from constantly restraining your authentic responses. Digestive issues, as your gut literally struggles to "digest" situations that don't feel right.

Frequent illness, as chronic stress suppresses immune function and leaves you vulnerable to every virus that comes around. Sleep disruption, as your mind races with worries about others' needs and your own neglected responsibilities. Muscle tension, particularly in the shoulders and neck, from carrying emotional weight that isn't yours to bear.

These aren't signs of weakness or poor health habits. They're signs of a body that's been pushed beyond its sustainable limits in service of maintaining relationships and avoiding conflict.

The Emotional Accumulation: The Resentment You Don't Want to Feel

Perhaps the most painful hidden cost of overgiving is the gradual accumulation of resentment. Not the kind you'd admit to anyone, including yourself. Not the dramatic, relationship-ending kind. But the quiet, persistent kind that builds like water behind a dam.

You don't want to feel resentful toward people you care about. You don't want to be angry at your family for needing you, your friends for asking for help, or your colleagues for depending on you. So you push the feelings down, minimize them, tell yourself you're being petty or ungrateful.

But resentment doesn't disappear when you ignore it. It goes underground, coloring your interactions in subtle ways. You might find yourself being a little less warm, a little more sarcastic, a little more tired in their presence. You give what's requested, but the joy has leaked out of the giving.

The Resentment Paradox Here's the cruel irony of overgiving: the very people you're trying to please often sense your resentment before you're willing to acknowledge it yourself. They might start walking on eggshells around you, or commenting that you seem "off" lately, or asking if something's wrong. This creates even more pressure to perform happiness, which deepens the resentment cycle.

Mark, a client who'd been the family problem-solver for years, described it this way: "I realized I was angry at them for taking advantage of my generosity, but I'd never told them where my limits were. I was resentful that they didn't appreciate my sacrifices, but I'd never explained what those sacrifices cost me. I was mad at them for a game where only I knew the rules."

The Self-Resentment Layer Even more damaging than feeling resentful toward others is the resentment you begin to feel toward yourself. You're angry at your inability to say no. Frustrated with your weakness in maintaining boundaries. Disgusted with your people-pleasing tendencies.

This self-resentment creates a vicious cycle: you overgive, feel resentful, judge yourself for feeling that way, then overgive again to prove you're not as selfish as your feelings suggest. Each cycle deepens the disconnection from your authentic self and reinforces the belief that your feelings aren't valid or important.

The Relational Erosion: How Overgiving Destroys What It's Trying to Protect

One of the most devastating hidden costs of overgiving is how it gradually erodes the very relationships you're trying to strengthen. While your intention is to show love through service, overgiving often creates unhealthy dynamics that leave both parties feeling unsatisfied.

The Dependency Creation When you consistently overgive, you inadvertently train others to become dependent on your excess capacity. They stop developing their own problem-solving skills because you're always there to solve problems for them. They stop considering your needs because you've shown them that you'll accommodate regardless.

This isn't usually conscious manipulation. It's human nature to take the path of least resistance. If someone is always willing to do the heavy lifting – emotionally, practically, or financially – most people will eventually let them.

Jennifer's Realization Jennifer, a successful marketing executive, spent years being the family's go-to person for everything from emergency babysitting to financial bailouts. She thought she was being loving and responsible.

"I realized I'd created a family of emotional teenagers," she told me. "They'd call me before thinking through their own solutions. They'd make plans assuming I'd be available to fill in the gaps. I thought I was helping them, but I was actually preventing them from growing up."

The turning point came when Jennifer went through her own crisis – a divorce that left her emotionally and financially drained. When she reached out for support, her family members were either unavailable or uncomfortable with the role reversal. "They'd become so used to me being the strong one that they didn't know how to be strong for me," she realized.

The Authenticity Erosion Overgiving also erodes authenticity in relationships. When you're always accommodating, always agreeable, always available, people don't get to know the real you. They know the version of you that serves their needs, but they miss your complexity, your struggles, your full humanity.

This creates what I call "functional relationships" – connections based on what you do rather than who you are. People value your role in their lives but don't really know your inner world. They appreciate your availability but remain unaware of your needs.

Over time, you might find yourself feeling lonely even in close relationships, because the version of you that others love isn't the complete you. It's the edited version that never complains, never needs anything, never creates inconvenience.

The Identity Erosion: Losing Yourself in Service

Perhaps the most insidious hidden cost of overgiving is the gradual loss of your sense of self. When your identity becomes organized around serving others, you can lose touch with your own preferences, opinions, and desires.

The Preference Paralysis Sarah, the client mentioned earlier, experienced what I call "preference paralysis" – the inability to know what you want when you've spent years focused exclusively on what others want. After decades of accommodating everyone else's choices, she found herself unable to answer simple questions about her own preferences.

"I went to a restaurant alone for the first time in years," she shared. "I sat there staring at the menu for twenty minutes because I literally didn't know what I wanted to eat. I'd become so used to asking others what they wanted, then choosing something that would work for everyone, that I'd lost touch with my own taste buds."

This extends beyond food choices to major life decisions. When you've spent years making choices based on others' needs, you can lose confidence in your own judgment and decision-making abilities.

The Opinion Vacuum Overgivers often experience what I call "opinion vacuum" – the gradual erosion of their own viewpoints through years of agreeing with others to maintain harmony. You might find yourself nodding along with conversations while thinking, "Do I even believe this? What do I actually think about this topic?"

This intellectual self-abandonment can leave you feeling like a fraud in conversations, uncertain of your own thoughts and uncomfortable expressing opinions that might create disagreement.

The Dream Deferral When you're constantly focused on enabling others' dreams and goals, your own aspirations often get indefinitely deferred. You tell yourself you'll pursue your interests "later," when things settle down, when others need you less, when you have more time.

But "later" often never comes, because the overgiving pattern doesn't naturally resolve itself. Instead, you might wake up years later wondering what happened to the dreams you put on hold.

The Spiritual Cost: Disconnection from Your Inner Wisdom

Beyond the physical, emotional, and relational costs, overgiving exacts a spiritual toll that's harder to quantify but equally damaging. When you consistently override your inner guidance to accommodate others, you gradually lose touch with your own wisdom and intuition.

The Internal Compass Confusion Your inner guidance system – the subtle feelings, instincts, and knowings that help you navigate life – depends on your willingness to listen to and honor these signals. When you repeatedly ignore your internal "no" to maintain external peace, you essentially teach yourself to distrust your own wisdom.

Over time, this creates what I call "internal compass confusion" – the inability to distinguish between what feels right and what feels obligatory. You might find yourself second-guessing decisions, seeking excessive external validation, or feeling generally unclear about your life direction.

The Authentic Expression Suppression Humans are creative beings with unique gifts, perspectives, and contributions to offer the world. When you're constantly molding yourself to meet others' expectations, your authentic expression gets suppressed. The world loses access to your particular brand of wisdom, creativity, and insight.

This suppression doesn't just affect you – it affects everyone who might have benefited from your authentic contributions. When you silence your voice to keep peace, everyone loses access to perspectives that might have been valuable, healing, or transformative.

The Compound Effect: How Small Costs Become Devastating

The individual costs of overgiving – a suppressed opinion here, an ignored boundary there, a deferred dream somewhere else – might seem manageable in isolation. But these costs compound over time, creating what I call the "overwhelm avalanche."

Like interest on debt, the costs of overgiving accumulate exponentially. The physical stress builds on itself. The emotional resentment deepens with each new episode. The relational imbalances become more entrenched. The identity erosion becomes more complete.

Eventually, you might reach what I call the "overgiving breaking point" – the moment when the accumulated costs become too heavy to carry. This might manifest as a health crisis, a relationship breakdown, an emotional collapse, or simply a quiet but profound realization that you can't continue living this way.

The Recovery Investment What many people don't realize is that recovering from chronic overgiving often requires significant time and energy investment. You have to rebuild your relationship with your body, learn to trust your emotions again, reconstruct authentic relationships, and rediscover your identity.

This recovery work is absolutely possible and worthwhile, but it requires resources. The irony is that many overgivers are so depleted from their giving that they struggle to find the energy needed for their own healing.

Recognizing the Hidden Costs in Your Life

The first step in addressing these hidden costs is honest recognition. Because overgiving often feels noble and virtuous, we tend to minimize or ignore its negative impacts. We tell ourselves we're just being helpful, that it's temporary, that we can handle it.

But your body and emotions are keeping track even when your mind isn't. Pay attention to:

Physical symptoms that don't have clear medical explanations. Emotional reactions that seem disproportionate to situations. Relationships that feel unbalanced or draining. A sense of disconnection from your own wants and needs. Chronic fatigue that rest doesn't resolve. Resentment that you feel guilty about having.

These aren't signs of weakness or character flaws. They're information. They're your system's way of communicating that something needs to change.

The Path Forward

Recognizing the hidden costs of overgiving isn't meant to create more guilt or self-criticism. It's meant to create motivation for change. When you understand what your current patterns are actually costing you, the prospect of transformation becomes not just appealing but necessary.

The costs we've explored in this chapter aren't permanent. Bodies can heal from chronic stress. Resentment can be resolved through honest communication and boundary-setting. Relationships can be rebalanced. Identity can be reclaimed. Spiritual connection can be restored.

But change begins with truth. And the truth is that overgiving, however well-intentioned, is not sustainable. It's not kind to you, and ultimately, it's not kind to the people you're trying to help.

In the next chapter, we'll begin exploring how to release the guilt that keeps these patterns in place. Because before you can create sustainable change, you need to address the emotional force that maintains the status quo: the belief that putting yourself first is selfish, wrong, or dangerous.

The costs of overgiving are real and significant. But so is your capacity to create something different. The journey toward sustainable kindness starts with honoring what your current patterns have truly cost you, and deciding that you're worth more than a life of depletion disguised as virtue.

Your body has been trying to tell you something important. It's time to listen.

CHAPTER 4

$$\perp$$

THE PERFORMANCE OF BEING "NICE"

I can still remember the exact moment I realized I'd been living as a character in my own life. I was at a dinner party, laughing at a joke I didn't find funny, nodding enthusiastically at an opinion I disagreed with, and offering to help clean up when I was exhausted and wanted to go home. As I stood in the kitchen washing dishes that weren't mine, smiling and chatting about topics that bored me, I had a startling thought: "Who is this person? And where did I go?"

That night marked the beginning of my understanding that there's a profound difference between being kind and being "nice." Kindness comes from an authentic place of care and flows naturally from who you are. Niceness, at least the way I'd been practicing it, was a performance – a carefully choreographed dance designed to ensure that everyone around me remained comfortable, regardless of how I felt.

The performance of being "nice" is perhaps the most exhausting show on earth, because it never ends. There's no intermission, no final curtain call, no moment when you get to step out of character and just be yourself. The show must go on, and you're always on stage.

The Theater of Niceness

Being perpetually "nice" requires you to become a skilled actor, constantly reading the room and adjusting your performance to match what others need from you. You develop an acute sensitivity to micro-expressions, vocal tones, and energy shifts, all in service of maintaining your role as the agreeable, helpful, low-maintenance person everyone can count on.

The Costume Department Like any good actor, you learn to dress for the part. Your facial expressions become carefully curated masks of pleasantness. Your voice takes on a particular tone – slightly higher, softer, more accommodating than your natural register. Your body language opens and yields, taking up less space, appearing less threatening or demanding.

Even your words become costumes. You develop a vocabulary of niceness: "Whatever you think is best," "I'm happy either way," "Don't worry about me," "I'm fine with anything." These phrases become so automatic that you might say them before you've even processed what you actually think or feel about the situation.

The Script Writing Over time, you become both actor and playwright, constantly writing scripts that cast you as the supporting character in everyone else's story. You rehearse conversations in advance, planning how to be helpful without being burdensome, how to express needs without seeming needy, how to disagree without being disagreeable.

You develop entire storylines about how considerate and understanding you are. You practice facial expressions in the mirror – the sympathetic nod, the encouraging smile, the concerned but not alarmed look of active listening. You become fluent in the language of deferral and accommodation.

The Method Acting Trap The most insidious aspect of the niceness performance is how convincing it becomes, even to yourself. Like method actors who lose themselves in their roles, you might begin to believe that the "nice" version of you is the real you. The performance becomes so seamless that you forget it's a performance at all.

This is when the real danger begins. When you can no longer distinguish between authentic kindness and performed niceness, you lose access to your genuine feelings, opinions, and desires. The character you've created to please others slowly eclipses the person you actually are.

The Exhaustion of Endless Performance

Emily came to me after what she called her "performance break-down" – a moment when she simply couldn't maintain the show anymore. "I was at my daughter's soccer game," she told me, "doing my usual thing – cheering for everyone, organizing snacks, making sure all the parents felt included. Then another mom asked me to coordinate the end-of-season party, and I just... broke. I started crying right there on the sidelines. Not sad crying, just complete overwhelm. I realized I'd been performing enthusiasm I didn't feel, energy I didn't have, and availability I couldn't sustain."

Emily's breakdown was actually a breakthrough. Her body and psyche had finally said "enough" to a performance that had been running non-stop for years.

The Physical Exhaustion Performing niceness is physically demanding in ways that aren't immediately obvious. Constantly monitoring and adjusting your facial expressions creates tension in your face and jaw. Modulating your voice to sound pleasant and agreeable strains your throat and breathing. Maintaining open, accommodating body language when you actually want to create boundaries exhausts your nervous system.

There's also the physical labor that often comes with being the "nice" person – you're the one who stays late to clean up, who brings extra food to events, who offers to drive people places, who helps with moving furniture or organizing activities. The performance of niceness often requires your body to do more work while pretending it's effortless.

The Emotional Labor Perhaps even more exhausting than the physical demands is the emotional labor of constant performance. You're perpetually managing not just your own emotions, but everyone else's. You become responsible for maintaining the mood of every room you enter, smoothing over awkward moments, diffusing tension, and ensuring that everyone feels comfortable.

This emotional choreography requires enormous mental energy. You're constantly running calculations: How is this person feeling? What do they need from me right now? How can I respond in a way that maintains harmony? What facial expression should I wear? What tone should I use?

The Cognitive Dissonance When your external performance consistently contradicts your internal experience, you create what psychologists call cognitive dissonance – the mental stress of holding contradictory beliefs or behaviors simultaneously. You smile while feeling annoyed, agree while disagreeing, offer help while feeling overwhelmed.

This dissonance is exhausting because your brain is constantly trying to reconcile the contradiction between what you're expressing and what you're experiencing. Over time, this mental gymnastics can lead to anxiety, depression, and a profound sense of disconnection from yourself.

The Audience You're Performing For

One of the most revealing questions I ask clients is: "Who exactly are you performing for?" The answers are often surprising, because the audience for niceness performance is rarely who you think it is.

The Invisible Critics Many people discover they're performing for an audience that isn't even present. They're being nice to avoid criticism from people who aren't there, to gain approval from individuals who may not even be paying attention, to prevent rejection from relationships that may not be as fragile as they imagine.

Marcus, a client who'd been performing niceness his entire adult life, had an revelation during one of our sessions: "I realized I was still performing for my critical father, who's been dead for ten years. I was being nice to coworkers because I was afraid they'd judge me the way he used to. I was accommodating friends because I was terrified they'd abandon me like he threatened to when I was a kid. I was performing for ghosts."

The Unappreciative Audience Even more heartbreaking is the realization that the people you're performing for often don't appreciate the show. In fact, they might prefer the authentic you to the performed version, but they've never met that person because you've been so committed to the character.

Sarah, the client we met earlier, made this discovery when she started being more authentic in her relationships: "I was shocked by how many people said they preferred the 'real' me. They said I seemed more interesting, more genuine, more fun to be around. I'd been working so hard to be likeable that I'd become boring. The performance wasn't even working."

The Enabling Audience Some people in your life have become accustomed to and dependent on your performance. They've grown comfortable with your endless accommodation, your consistent availability, your perpetual agreeableness. For these audience members, your authentic self might feel threatening because it challenges the dynamic they've come to expect.

This is perhaps the most difficult aspect of stopping the performance – some people won't like it. They've benefited from your self-sacrifice and may resist changes that require them to be more considerate, more self-sufficient, or more reciprocal in the relationship.

The Script vs. The Spontaneous

Authentic kindness is spontaneous. It arises naturally from genuine care and flows in response to real situations. It's specific, timely, and proportionate to what's actually needed. Most importantly, it comes from a place of abundance rather than fear.

Performed niceness, by contrast, is scripted. It follows predictable patterns regardless of the situation. It's more about maintaining your image as a nice person than responding authentically to what's happening in the moment.

The Difference in Action Let me illustrate with a simple example. Imagine a friend tells you they're going through a difficult time:

Performed niceness response: "Oh no! What can I do to help? Do you need me to come over? I can bring dinner, or help with errands, or just listen. Whatever you need, I'm here for you. Don't worry about me – I'm totally free and happy to help in any way."

Authentic kindness response: "I'm sorry you're going through this. How are you feeling about it?" (Pauses to actually listen) "I care about you and want to support you. I could bring dinner Thursday if that would help, or we could talk on the phone tomorrow evening when I have time to really focus. What would feel most helpful to you right now?"

The difference is subtle but profound. The performed response is immediate, excessive, and focused on proving your niceness. The authentic response is thoughtful, specific, and focused on genuinely understanding and meeting the person's needs within your actual capacity.

The Quality of Presence When you're performing niceness, part of your attention is always on the performance itself – monitoring how you're coming across, whether you're saying the right things, whether you're being nice enough. This divided attention means you're never fully present with the person you're trying to help.

Authentic kindness allows for complete presence because you're not managing a performance. You can listen more deeply, respond more accurately, and offer help that's actually useful rather than just visibly generous.

The Social Reinforcement Trap

One reason the performance of niceness becomes so entrenched is that society actively rewards it, especially in certain groups. "Nice" people get praised, promoted, and preferred. They're seen as team players, good friends, and reliable family members.

This social reinforcement creates what I call the "niceness addiction" – a dependency on external validation that comes from being perceived as endlessly giving and accommodating. Like any addiction, it requires increasing doses to maintain the same high, leading to more extreme acts of self-sacrifice and accommodation.

The Gender Trap This trap is particularly insidious for women, who are often socialized from birth to prioritize others' comfort over their own authenticity. "Be nice," "be sweet," "be helpful," "don't be difficult" – these messages shape many women into chronic performers who lose touch with their genuine selves in pursuit of being liked.

But men aren't immune. They might perform niceness differently – through being the reliable provider, the problem-solver, the strong shoulder to lean on – but the underlying dynamic is the same: sacrificing authenticity for approval.

The Professional Performance The workplace often demands and rewards performed niceness, especially in service industries, healthcare, education, and other people-focused fields. Being "nice" becomes part of the job description, and the line between professional courtesy and personal authenticity becomes increasingly blurred.

Many people find themselves performing niceness at work for eight hours a day, then struggling to turn it off when they go home. The performance becomes so habitual that they lose access to their authentic responses even in personal relationships.

When Others Can Sense the Performance

Here's something that might surprise you: people can often tell when your kindness is performed rather than authentic. Humans are remarkably sensitive to genuine emotion versus manufactured responses. While they might not be able to articulate what feels "off," they often sense when someone is acting rather than being.

The Uncanny Valley of Niceness Just as CGI characters can look almost human but feel unsettling because they're not quite right, performed niceness can feel unsettling to recipients because it's not quite authentic. The timing might be slightly off, the responses too perfect, the eagerness a bit too intense.

People might find themselves feeling uncomfortable around you without knowing why. They might sense that they're not getting the real you, which can actually create the very distance and dis-connection you're trying to prevent through your performance.

The Relationship Impact Ironically, the performance of niceness often creates the opposite of what it's intended to achieve. Instead of deeper connections, you get functional relationships. Instead of love, you get appreciation for your usefulness. Instead of authentic intimacy, you get surface-level pleasantness.

Many chronic performers discover that when they finally drop the act and start being genuine, their relationships actually improve. The people who truly care about them prefer the authentic ver-sion, even if it's more complex and less accommodating than the performed version.

The Moment the Performance Breaks Down

For most people, there comes a moment when the performance simply can't be sustained anymore. This might happen gradually — a slow erosion of your ability to maintain the act — or sud-denly, in what feels like a complete breakdown of your niceness façade.

The Breaking Point Jennifer, a social worker who'd been per-forming niceness for twenty years, described her breaking point: "I was at a family gathering, doing my usual thing – helping in the kitchen, mediating conflicts, making sure everyone was happy. Then my aunt made a passive-aggressive comment about my divorce, and instead of smiling and changing the subject like I always did, I just... stopped. I looked at her and said, 'That was unkind.' The whole room went quiet. I realized I'd never once challenged anyone's behavior because I was so committed to being the nice one.'"

That moment of authenticity felt terrifying to Jennifer, but it was also liberating. "I realized I'd been enabling bad behavior by never calling it out. I wasn't actually being kind by letting people treat me poorly. I was just being convenient."

The Recovery Process Recovering from chronic niceness performance isn't simple, because the performance has often become so integrated into your identity that you're not sure who you are without it. You might fear that if you're not constantly nice, people won't like you, or worse, that you'll discover you're actually selfish or mean.

The recovery process involves gradually reconnecting with your authentic responses while learning to distinguish between genuine kindness and performed accommodation. It's about finding the person underneath the performance and discovering that your authentic self is actually more likeable, more interesting, and more genuinely caring than the character you've been playing.

The Freedom of Authenticity

When you finally stop performing niceness and start expressing authentic kindness, something remarkable happens: you discover that being genuine is far less exhausting than being perpetually agreeable.

Authentic responses require no rehearsal, no monitoring, no adjustment. They flow naturally from who you are in the moment. You can disagree without being disagreeable, set boundaries without being cruel, and care for others without sacrificing yourself.

The Energy Shift Maria, who we met in earlier chapters, described the energy shift this way: "I used to come home from social events completely drained because I'd been 'on' the whole time. Now I come home energized, even from challenging conversations, because I was actually present instead of performing. It turns out that authenticity is energizing while performance is depleting."

The Relationship Shift When you stop performing niceness, you also create space for others to be authentic with you. The artificial pleasantness that characterized your interactions gets replaced by genuine connection. You might have fewer relationships, but the ones you maintain are deeper, more honest, and more fulfilling.

Recognizing Your Own Performance

If you've recognized yourself in this chapter, you might be wondering how to tell the difference between authentic kindness and performed niceness in your own life. Here are some questions that can help:

Do you feel energized or drained after being "nice"? Authentic kindness usually feels good, while performed niceness feels depleting.

Are you responding to what's actually needed, or to what you think you should provide? Authentic kindness is responsive to real needs, while performed niceness follows scripts.

Can you easily say no when you don't want to help, or do you feel compelled to say yes? Authentic kindness includes the ability to decline gracefully.

Do you feel resentful after helping, or genuinely good about your contribution? Resentment is often a sign that the kindness was performed rather than freely given.

Are you being kind because you want to, or because you're afraid of what will happen if you don't? Authentic kindness comes from desire, while performed niceness comes from fear.

The Beginning of the End

Recognizing that you've been performing niceness rather than expressing authentic kindness can feel devastating at first. You might wonder who you really are underneath all that accommodation. You might fear that without the performance, you'll be selfish, difficult, or unlikeable.

But this recognition is actually the beginning of freedom. It's the first step toward discovering your authentic self and learning to express genuine care from a place of choice rather than compulsion.

The performance of being "nice" is exhausting because it's not sustainable. No one can maintain a character indefinitely without losing touch with who they really are. But authentic kindness – kindness that flows from your genuine nature rather than your fears – is infinitely renewable because it comes from truth rather than effort.

In the chapters that follow, we'll explore how to recognize these performance patterns in your daily life, examine the beliefs that maintain them, and gradually release the guilt and fear that keep the show running. Because the goal isn't to become less caring – it's to become more authentically kind.

The curtain is about to fall on your niceness performance. And when it does, you'll discover that the person you've been hiding behind all that agreeableness is far more interesting, more genuinely caring, and more worthy of love than the character you've been playing.

The real you has been waiting in the wings long enough. It's time to let them take center stage.

CHAPTER 5

RECOGNIZE THE PATTERN

The first time I tracked my overgiving for a week, I expected to find random acts of kindness scattered throughout my days. What I discovered instead was a pattern so precise it could have been programmed by a computer.

Monday morning at 9:15 AM: colleague mentions being swamped, I immediately offer to help with her presentation. Tuesday at lunch: friend seems down, I spend my entire break listening and giving advice. Wednesday evening: family group text about holiday planning turns tense, I volunteer to coordinate everything. Thursday night: neighbor asks if I can watch their dog this weekend, I say yes despite having my own plans.

By Friday, I was exhausted and inexplicably angry at everyone I'd helped. But when I looked at my notes, the pattern was undeniable. I wasn't randomly being helpful – I was following a script I didn't even know I'd memorized.

That week of tracking changed everything. For the first time, I could see that my overgiving wasn't a character flaw or a series of unfortunate coincidences. It was a predictable response to specific triggers, as automatic as pulling your hand away from a hot stove.

The Three-Part Pattern

Every overgiving episode follows the same basic structure: something happens (the trigger), you respond in a predictable way (the response), and you get something from it that keeps the pattern alive (the payoff). Understanding this cycle is like having a map to your own behavior.

Jenna's Discovery Jenna, a marketing director and mother of two, came to me completely bewildered by her own behavior. "I keep saying yes to things I don't want to do," she said. "Last week alone, I agreed to organize the school fundraiser, help my sister move, and take on an extra project at work. I have no idea why I keep doing this to myself."

We spent our first session mapping out just one of these episodes in detail. Her sister had called, sounding stressed about finding movers. Within minutes, Jenna had offered to help pack, recruit friends to assist, and even provide lunch for everyone.

"What were you feeling right before you offered to help?" I asked.

Jenna paused, thinking back. "My sister sounded so overwhelmed. I felt this surge of anxiety, like something terrible would happen if I didn't jump in. And then when I offered to help and heard the relief in her voice... I felt so much better. Like I'd prevented a disaster."

That's when Jenna saw her pattern clearly for the first time: anxiety about others' distress (trigger), immediate rescue offering (response), relief and sense of importance (payoff). Once she recognized this cycle, she began noticing it everywhere in her life.

Over the following weeks, Jenna discovered that her pattern wasn't limited to family crises. Any time someone around her seemed stressed or struggling, she'd feel that same surge of anxiety and immediately jump into fix-it mode. Colleagues mentioning workload issues, friends dealing with relationship problems, even strangers at the grocery store who seemed lost – all triggered her automatic rescue response.

"I realized I'd become a professional anxiety-absorber," she said. "I was more tuned into other people's stress levels than my own. The moment I sensed someone struggling, my nervous system would activate like I was personally responsible for solving their problems."

The Trigger Recognition

Your triggers are like alarm bells that activate your overgiving response. Some are external – situations or people that seem to need your help. Others are internal – emotions or thoughts that make you feel compelled to act.

Lisa's Emotional Radar Lisa, a social worker who'd been overgiving her entire adult life, discovered that her triggers were primarily emotional. She had what she called "superhuman empathy radar" – an almost painful sensitivity to others' discomfort that made her immediately want to intervene.

"I could walk into a room and instantly sense the emotional temperature," she explained. "If there was any tension, sadness, or conflict, I'd feel it in my body like a physical alarm. My chest would get tight, my shoulders would tense up, and I'd feel this overwhelming urge to do something – anything – to make it better."

This emotional sensitivity had served Lisa well in her professional life, but it was destroying her personal relationships. Family dinners became exhausting performances where she mediated every disagreement and smoothed over every awkward moment. Social gatherings turned into work as she managed everyone's emotional state.

The turning point came during a family barbecue where her brother and father got into a heated discussion about politics. Lisa immediately jumped in with jokes and subject changes, trying to defuse the tension. But her teenage nephew pulled her aside afterward and said, "Aunt Lisa, why don't you ever let people just talk through their disagreements? Sometimes conflict is okay."

That comment stopped Lisa cold. She realized she'd been treating all emotional discomfort as an emergency that required her intervention. "I couldn't tolerate anyone being upset, angry, or uncomfortable for even a moment," she said. "But I was robbing them of the chance to work through their own feelings and resolve their own conflicts."

The Response Patterns

Once triggered, most people have signature responses – specific ways they consistently overgive. You might be an advice-giver, a task-taker, a mediator, or a rescuer. Your response pattern is often so automatic you might not realize you're doing it.

David's Automatic Solutions David, an engineer who approached problems with the same methodical precision he used at work, discovered that his signature response was immediate problem-solving. The moment someone mentioned any difficulty, his brain would shift into solution mode.

"My wife would say she was tired, and I'd suggest vitamins, sleep apps, and offer to reorganize her schedule," he said. "My friend would mention work stress, and I'd research career coaching options and present him with a whole action plan. My teenage daughter would complain about friend drama, and I'd outline communication strategies like I was giving a presentation."

David thought he was being helpful and supportive. But his family started avoiding sharing problems with him because they felt overwhelmed by his immediate solutions. "My wife finally told me that sometimes she just wanted me to listen and say 'that sounds hard' instead of trying to fix everything," he said.

This feedback initially confused David. Why wouldn't someone want solutions to their problems? But as he began paying attention to his automatic response, he realized that his immediate problem-solving often prevented people from processing their own feelings or developing their own solutions.

"I was treating everyone like they were broken computers that needed debugging," he realized. "I wasn't actually listening to what they needed – I was just running my own program of fix-first-ask-questions-later."

When David learned to pause before offering solutions, he discovered that most people already knew what they needed to do. They weren't looking for his engineering expertise – they were looking for understanding and support while they figured things out themselves.

The Hidden Payoffs

The most important part of recognizing your pattern is understanding what you get from it. This might feel uncomfortable to admit, because we don't like to think we have ulterior motives for helping others. But every behavior that persists has some kind of payoff, even if it's unconscious.

Jenna discovered that her rescue pattern provided multiple payoffs: immediate relief from anxiety, a sense of importance and value, and insurance against abandonment. "When I helped my sister, I felt needed and appreciated. It confirmed that I was a good person and a valuable family member," she said.

Lisa realized that her emotional management gave her a sense of control in situations that otherwise felt chaotic. "I couldn't control whether people got upset, but I could control my response to their upset. Managing everyone's emotions made me feel useful and important," she explained.

David found that his problem-solving boosted his sense of competence and expertise. "I felt smart and capable when I could quickly analyze someone's situation and offer solutions. It was like getting a little hit of professional validation in my personal relationships," he admitted.

Understanding these payoffs wasn't about judging themselves harshly. It was about recognizing the hidden functions their overgiving served so they could find healthier ways to meet those legitimate needs.

The Real-Time Recognition

Once you understand your pattern intellectually, the next step is catching it in action. This requires what I call "pattern mindfulness" – a gentle awareness of your internal state and automatic responses as they happen.

Lisa learned to recognize the physical sensation that preceded her emotional management episodes. "I'd feel this tightness in my chest when tension appeared in a room," she said. "My shoulders would go up, and I'd get this urge to move into action. Once I learned to notice that physical response, I could pause and ask myself whether intervention was actually needed or if I was just uncomfortable with the conflict."

David discovered that his problem-solving mode had a distinct mental feeling. "My brain would start racing, generating solutions faster than the person could even finish describing their problem," he said. "Learning to notice that mental acceleration helped me slow down and actually listen instead of immediately jumping to fix mode."

The goal isn't to immediately stop all helping behavior. It's to create a tiny space between your trigger and your response – just enough time to make a conscious choice rather than following your automatic pattern.

This pause can be as simple as taking three deep breaths before responding to a request for help. Or asking, "Can I think about this and get back to you?" instead of immediately saying yes. The pause doesn't have to be long – just long enough to engage your conscious mind rather than your automatic response.

The Pattern Evolution

Understanding your patterns is an ongoing process, not a one-time insight. As you become more aware of them, they'll begin to evolve and change. Some patterns will fade naturally once you recognize them. Others will require more conscious effort to interrupt and reshape.

Jennifer's Journey Jennifer, a teacher who'd been chronically over-extended in both her professional and personal life, tracked her patterns for six months and watched them evolve in fascinating ways.

"At first, I was just catching them after the fact – noticing that I'd overgiven again and feeling frustrated," she said. "I'd agree to cover extra classes, volunteer for committees I had no time for, and take on everyone's emotional problems, then wonder why I was so exhausted."

"Then I started catching them in the moment, which felt like progress even though I still went through with the helping. I'd notice myself saying yes to things I didn't want to do, but I felt powerless to change course mid-conversation."

"Eventually, I began noticing the triggers before the pattern fully activated. That's when I could actually make different choices. Now, several months later, I still help people all the time, but it's conscious helping rather than compulsive helping. The difference in how it feels is extraordinary."

Jennifer's transformation didn't happen overnight, but each stage built on the previous one. Recognition led to awareness, awareness led to choice, and choice led to genuine freedom in her relationships with others.

Your Personal Investigation

Recognizing your patterns requires becoming a compassionate detective in your own life. For one week, simply notice:

When do you find yourself automatically offering help? What was happening right before – both externally in the situation and internally in your emotional state? How do you feel immediately after helping someone? How do you feel about it several hours later?

Don't try to change anything during this week. Just gather information with curiosity rather than judgment. Your patterns developed for good reasons and have likely served important functions in your life.

The goal of pattern recognition isn't to stop caring about others or to become selfish. It's to make your kindness conscious, sustainable, and genuinely beneficial for everyone involved. When you can see your patterns clearly, you can begin to understand what maintains them and ultimately choose responses that serve your authentic values rather than your unconscious fears.

In the next chapter, we'll explore the deeper beliefs that keep these patterns alive – the fundamental assumptions about yourself, others, and relationships that make overgiving feel not just appropriate, but necessary for survival.

CHAPTER 6

EXAMINE THE BELIEFS

The email arrived at 2 AM on a Sunday. Sarah's colleague needed help with a project due Monday morning—something that could have been handled weeks earlier with proper planning. Sarah found herself reaching for her laptop, fingers already typing a response offering to spend her weekend fixing someone else's crisis.

Then she stopped.

For the first time in her adult life, she asked herself a simple question: *Why do I feel like I have to say yes?*

The answer that surfaced surprised her: "Because good people don't have needs."

That belief had been running her life for thirty-seven years, and she'd never questioned it once.

The Hidden Operating System

What Sarah discovered that night was what I call the "invisible architecture" of overgiving—the fundamental beliefs that drive our behavior from beneath conscious awareness. Your overgiving patterns aren't random habits or personality quirks. They're the logical expression of deeply held assumptions about yourself, others, and how relationships work.

These beliefs operate like the foundation of a house—invisible but absolutely essential to everything built on top of them. You can rearrange the furniture (your behaviors) all you want, but if the foundation is cracked, the house will never be stable.

Most of us never examine our beliefs about kindness, worth, and relationships because they feel like facts rather than opinions. They're often formed early in life, reinforced by family dynamics, cultural messages, and personal experiences until they become part of our mental operating system.

Reflection Question: What beliefs about helping others do you hold so deeply that they feel like universal truths?

The Belief Behind Every Pattern

Every overgiving pattern is powered by at least one core belief that makes the behavior feel not just reasonable, but absolutely necessary. Rebecca, a successful lawyer who'd been chronically overextended since childhood, discovered that her people-pleasing was driven by the belief that "love is conditional on performance."

She'd learned this lesson young when her parents' affection seemed to fluctuate based on her achievements and helpfulness. Good grades and helpful behavior earned warmth and attention. Struggles or typical childhood needs resulted in emotional withdrawal.

"I thought everyone was keeping score," Rebecca told me. "I believed that if I wasn't constantly proving my worth through what I did for others, they'd discover I wasn't worth keeping around. It never occurred to me that people might value me for who I am rather than what I provide."

This belief had been so fundamental to Rebecca's worldview that she'd never questioned it. It felt like a law of nature rather than a learned assumption. But once she could see it clearly, she began to notice how it influenced every relationship in her life—and more importantly, how she might choose differently.

When Noble Principles Hide Complex Motivations

Our beliefs about overgiving often disguise themselves as admirable principles, making them particularly difficult to challenge. After all, who wants to argue against being helpful, considerate, or selfless?

The Virtue Trap

Michael, a pastor who'd been burning himself out in service to his congregation, initially resisted examining his motivations. "Isn't selfless service what we're called to do?" he asked. "Doesn't questioning my motives make me selfish?"

When we explored deeper, Michael discovered that his "selfless" service was actually driven by terror of being seen as inadequate. He believed that if he wasn't constantly available, endlessly giving, and perpetually self-sacrificing, he'd be exposed as a fraud who didn't deserve his position.

"I realized I wasn't serving God or my congregation," he said. "I was serving my own fear of being found out. My overgiving was actually the most selfish thing I could do because it was all about managing my anxiety rather than truly caring for others."

Self-Assessment: When you feel compelled to help someone, pause and ask: "Am I responding to their need or to my own discomfort with not helping?"

The Efficiency Excuse

Other people frame their overgiving in practical terms: "It's easier if I just do it myself," "I'm good at managing these things," "Someone has to take care of this." These statements might be factually accurate, but they often mask deeper beliefs about responsibility and control.

Anna, a small business owner who personally managed every detail of her company and family life, believed she was just being efficient. But underneath that practical narrative was a conviction that disaster would strike if she wasn't personally overseeing everything.

"I thought I was being responsible," she said. "But I was actually operating from a belief that no one else could be trusted to handle important things correctly. I was micromanaging everyone in my life because I believed that anything less than my constant oversight would lead to failure."

This realization opened a crucial question: Was Anna's hyper-responsibility protecting others, or was it actually limiting their growth and her own freedom?

The Three Pillars of Overgiving Beliefs

While everyone's specific beliefs are unique, most overgiving patterns are built on variations of three fundamental assumptions. Understanding these categories can help you identify which beliefs might be driving your own behavior.

Pillar One: Beliefs About Your Worth

These beliefs determine how you think you earn value and maintain your place in relationships. Perhaps you've internalized the idea that your worth depends entirely on what you do for others, or that you're only valuable when you're actively useful. Maybe you feel that if you're not constantly giving, you must be taking too much, or that love must be earned through endless service. Some people carry the heavy assumption that their needs inherently make them a burden to others.

Sarah, the emergency room nurse we met earlier, traced her overgiving to a childhood where she'd learned that love was earned through caretaking. As the eldest of five children with an overwhelmed single mother, Sarah had discovered that the surest way to get positive attention was to help with her younger siblings.

"I learned that being helpful made me valuable," she said. "But I also learned that having needs of my own made me part of the problem. So I became really good at anticipating what others needed while completely ignoring what I needed."

Challenge Exercise: For one week, notice when you feel most valued by others. Is it when you're helping, or are there other moments when you feel appreciated simply for being yourself?

Pillar Two: Beliefs About Others

These beliefs shape how you see other people's capabilities and needs. You might assume that others simply can't handle their problems without your direct intervention, or that people will inevitably be hurt or angry if you don't rush to help them. Perhaps you've concluded that everyone else's needs are inherently more important than your own, or that the people in your life are fundamentally fragile and require your constant protection. Many overgivers live with the deep fear that people will abandon them if they're not perpetually helpful and available.

Thomas, a middle school teacher who'd been overextending himself for years, discovered that his rescue pattern was driven by beliefs about others' fragility. He couldn't see a colleague struggling without immediately offering solutions, resources, or direct assistance.

"I treated everyone like they were my students," he realized. "I assumed they needed my guidance and support to handle their challenges. But most of them were competent adults who were perfectly capable of managing their own problems. My 'help' was actually kind of insulting because it implied they couldn't handle their own lives."

Pillar Three: Beliefs About Relationships

These beliefs determine how you think healthy connections work. You might believe that any conflict signals imminent relationship danger, or that good relationships require constant, unbroken harmony. Perhaps you've convinced yourself that having boundaries will inevitably drive people away, or that genuine love means never saying no to anyone you care about. Some people operate from the assumption that healthy relationships are fundamentally unbalanced, with one person perpetually giving while the other receives.

Maria, a marketing executive who'd been the family peacekeeper since childhood, believed that any conflict signaled relationship failure. This belief made her hypervigilant about tension and compulsively driven to restore harmony at any cost.

"I thought love meant never disagreeing," she said. "I believed that if people truly cared about each other, they'd avoid anything that might cause conflict. So I became a professional conflict-avoider, always smoothing things over and never expressing opinions that might create friction."

The cost was enormous: Maria's relationships felt surface-level because she never shared her authentic thoughts or feelings when they might create disagreement. People appreciated her agreeableness, but no one really knew who she was underneath all that accommodation.

Relationship Audit: Think about your closest relationships. How much of your authentic self—including disagreements, needs, and boundaries—do you actually share?

The Origins of Overgiving Beliefs

Understanding where your beliefs came from isn't about blame or making excuses. It's about recognizing that these assumptions developed in specific contexts where they may have been adaptive or even necessary for survival.

Family Laboratory Lessons

Many overgiving beliefs are learned in childhood through direct teaching or careful observation. You might have grown up in a family where love was conditional on helpfulness, where conflict felt dangerous, or where emotional needs were treated as weaknesses.

Rebecca's belief that "love is conditional on performance" developed in a household where her parents' attention and affection clearly correlated with her achievements. The message was subtle but consistent: be helpful and successful, receive love; struggle or need support, face emotional withdrawal.

"I learned to read my parents' moods and adjust my behavior accordingly," she said. "If they seemed stressed, I'd become extra helpful. If they seemed happy, I'd work to maintain that happiness.

I became a little emotional manager, constantly monitoring and responding to their needs while learning to hide my own."

Cultural Programming

Our broader culture also teaches beliefs about kindness, selflessness, and relationships. Messages about gender roles, religious duty, professional expectations, and social responsibility all shape our assumptions about how much we should give and what we should expect in return.

These cultural scripts can be particularly powerful because they're reinforced everywhere—in media, religious communities, workplaces, and social interactions. Many women receive explicit and implicit messages that their value lies in nurturing others. Many men learn that their worth comes from providing and protecting. Professional environments often reward endless availability and accommodation.

Survival Adaptations

Sometimes overgiving beliefs develop as adaptations to traumatic or unstable environments. If caregiving was the only way to feel safe, valuable, or connected during difficult periods, these beliefs might have been literally life-saving at the time.

Anna's belief that "I have to manage everything or disaster will strike" developed during a chaotic childhood with an alcoholic parent. Taking responsibility for household management, younger siblings, and even her parent's emotional state had been a survival strategy.

"Being hyperresponsible wasn't just helpful—it was necessary," she said. "Someone had to keep things together, and I learned that someone was me. The belief that I had to manage everything wasn't wrong in that context. It just stopped serving me when I carried it into adult relationships with functional people."

Breaking the Belief-Behavior Loop

Once established, beliefs and behaviors reinforce each other in a continuous cycle. Your beliefs drive your overgiving behaviors, and your overgiving behaviors seem to confirm your beliefs, making them feel increasingly true and necessary.

If you believe that "people will leave if I'm not constantly helpful," you'll engage in constant helpfulness. When people appreciate your help and maintain the relationship, it appears to confirm that your helpfulness is what keeps them around. You never get to test whether they'd stay anyway because you never stop helping long enough to find out.

This creates what psychologists call a "confirmatory bias loop"—you only gather evidence that supports your existing beliefs while avoiding situations that might challenge them.

The Art of Belief Testing

The way to interrupt this loop is to start questioning whether your beliefs are actually true in your current relationships and circumstances. This doesn't mean recklessly abandoning all helpful behavior, but rather conducting small, safe experiments to test whether your beliefs hold up under scrutiny.

Sarah began testing her belief that "my worth depends on what I do for others" by occasionally letting others handle their own problems without her intervention. To her surprise, most people managed fine without her help, and their appreciation for her didn't decrease. In fact, some relationships actually improved because people felt more respected and capable.

"I realized I'd been underestimating everyone," she said. "I thought they needed my constant help to function, but they were actually quite capable. My belief wasn't protecting them—it was limiting them."

Belief Testing Exercise: Choose one small belief to test this week. For example, if you believe "people will be upset if I don't immediately respond to their texts," try waiting an hour before responding and observe what actually happens.

From Unconscious to Conscious

The goal isn't to adopt a completely new set of assumptions overnight. It's to move from unconscious, automatic beliefs to conscious, chosen ones. This means regularly asking yourself: Do I still believe this? Is this belief serving me and my relationships? What evidence do I have for and against this assumption?

Maria's journey with her conflict-avoidance belief illustrates this process beautifully. Instead of automatically assuming that disagreement meant relationship danger, she began experimenting with small conflicts to test her assumption.

"I started expressing minor disagreements about things like restaurant choices or movie preferences," she said. "To my amazement, these small conflicts actually seemed to make my relationships more interesting and authentic. People appreciated getting to know my real opinions instead of just my agreeable responses."

Over time, Maria developed a more nuanced belief: "Some conflict is healthy and can actually strengthen relationships when handled respectfully." This conscious belief allowed her to engage more authentically while still maintaining her natural consideration for others.

The Freedom of Conscious Choice

When you can see your beliefs clearly and choose which ones to keep, you gain the freedom to respond to situations based on current reality rather than old assumptions. This doesn't mean becoming selfish or uncaring—it means being intentionally kind rather than compulsively accommodating.

Thomas discovered that his belief about others' fragility had developed during a period when he was genuinely surrounded by people who needed significant support. But he'd generalized this belief to all relationships, continuing to treat competent adults like fragile students who needed his constant guidance.

"The belief wasn't wrong in the context where it developed," he said. "But I was applying it inappropriately to new situations. Learning to see people as capable adults rather than fragile children transformed my relationships completely."

Integration Practice: At the end of each day for the next week, ask yourself: "Which of my actions today came from conscious choice, and which came from unconscious beliefs?"

Moving Forward

Your beliefs about kindness, worth, and relationships will continue to evolve throughout your life. The goal isn't to find the "perfect" set of beliefs but to remain conscious about the assumptions that drive your behavior. When you can see the invisible architecture of your choices, you can build relationships and a life that truly reflects your values rather than your fears.

Remember: questioning your beliefs isn't about becoming less caring—it's about caring more consciously and effectively. The world needs your kindness, but it needs it to come from a place of strength and choice rather than fear and compulsion.

In the next chapter, we'll explore how to release the guilt that often accompanies changing these long-held beliefs and behaviors. Because even when you intellectually understand that your beliefs might be limiting you, guilt can keep you trapped in old patterns. Learning to release this guilt is essential for creating lasting change.

CHAPTER 7

LET GO OF GUILT

I was six years old when my mother noticed me clutching my favorite toy truck in the corner of the playground. Another child had been eyeing it, clearly wanting a turn, but I held it tighter against my chest.

"Give the child a turn," my mother said firmly. "You'll get it back."

I didn't want to share. The truck was mine; I was still playing with it, and it felt like I should get to decide whether I wanted to share my toy or not. But my mother's disapproval felt bigger than my feelings. I respected her, and disappointing her seemed worse than giving up what I wanted. Reluctantly, I handed over the truck.

The other child immediately ran off with it to the far side of the playground. I never got it back that day.

More than three decades later, that moment still haunts me. Not because of the lost toy, but because of the lesson I absorbed: wanting to keep something for myself was selfish. Saying no to someone else's needs or wants made me a bad person. That day taught me to feel guilty about having boundaries, and that guilt has followed me everywhere since. Whether it's the last bite of food on my plate, the money in my wallet, or simply my time and energy, this guilt has followed me everywhere.

Even now, when a friend eyes my dessert or a colleague asks for a loan, I feel that same six-year-old shame creeping in. The guilt hits me like a physical blow, whispering that keeping anything for myself is wrong, that good people always give and that my own needs and boundaries are inherently selfish.

That childhood guilt became the guardian of my adult overgiving patterns. It was the emotional force that kept me trapped in cycles of endless accommodation, even when I intellectually understood they weren't serving me. Learning to recognize and release this guilt became essential for creating lasting change.

The Difference Between Guilt and Regret

Guilt is perhaps the most misunderstood emotion when it comes to changing overgiving patterns. Many people think guilt is their moral compass, warning them when they're being selfish or uncaring. But there's a crucial difference between healthy regret and toxic guilt.

Healthy regret says, "I wish I'd handled that differently. I can learn from this and make a better choice next time." It's specific, proportionate, and focused on behavior rather than identity.

Toxic guilt says, "I'm a terrible person for prioritizing myself. I should always put others first, regardless of the cost to me." It's global, disproportionate, and attacks your character rather than addressing specific actions.

Elena's Guilt Journey Elena, a nurse practitioner who'd been overextending herself for years, experienced this distinction firsthand when she started setting boundaries with colleagues who constantly asked her to cover their shifts.

"The first time I said no to covering a Saturday shift, I felt sick with guilt," she told me. "I kept imagining the unit being short-staffed, patients not getting proper care, and my colleagues thinking I was selfish and unreliable."

But when Elena examined these thoughts more closely, she realized they were based on catastrophic assumptions rather than reality. The hospital had protocols for staffing shortages. Her colleagues were capable professionals who could handle the situation. Her one "no" didn't make her selfish or unreliable.

"I realized the guilt wasn't about actual harm I was causing," she said. "It was about violating an internal rule I didn't even know I had: that good nurses never say no, that my worth depended on my constant availability, and that setting boundaries was inherently selfish."

The Origins of Overgiving Guilt

Understanding where your guilt comes from helps you evaluate whether it's providing useful information or simply enforcing outdated patterns.

Family Guilt Messages Many people learn to feel guilty about self-care from families where individual needs were seen as selfish or where love was conditional on self-sacrifice. You might have received explicit messages like "good children put family first" or absorbed implicit lessons through watching the family dynamics.

Marcus grew up in a household where his mother's constant self-sacrifice was praised as the highest virtue. She never took time for herself, never expressed personal needs, and frequently commented on how "selfish" people were who prioritized their own wants.

"I learned that goodness was measured by how much you gave up for others," Marcus said. "Taking care of myself felt morally wrong because I'd been taught that self-focus was selfishness. The guilt

I felt when setting boundaries wasn't my conscience; it was my mother's voice telling me I was being bad."

Cultural Guilt Programming Broader cultural messages also shape our guilt responses. Many cultures, religions, and communities have strong narratives about self-sacrifice, service, and putting others first. While these values can inspire beautiful generosity, they can also create guilt about normal human needs for rest, boundaries, and self-care.

Women often receive particularly intense cultural messages about selflessness, while men might feel guilty about not being strong enough to handle everyone's problems. Religious communities sometimes conflate godliness with endless giving. Professional environments may cultivate guilt about work-life balance.

Trauma-Based Guilt Sometimes guilt about self-care develops as a response to trauma or neglect. If your needs were consistently dismissed, minimized, or punished, you might have learned to feel guilty for having them at all.

Sarah, whose mother struggled with severe depression, learned as a child that expressing her needs felt cruel when her mother was barely functioning. "I felt guilty for wanting attention, help with homework, or even basic care," she said. "It seemed selfish to need things when my mom was suffering so much."

This childhood dynamic created a lasting pattern where Sarah felt guilty any time she prioritized her own needs, even in completely unrelated adult relationships.

The Guilt Spiral

Guilt about setting boundaries often creates a vicious cycle that reinforces overgiving patterns. Here's how it typically works:

You start to set a boundary or prioritize yourself, guilt kicks in and tells you you're being selfish, you override the boundary to relieve the guilt, you feel temporary relief but long-term resentment, the resentment makes you feel even more guilty for being ungrateful, you overcompensate by giving even more.

Breaking the Spiral Rachel, a social worker who'd been trapped in this cycle for years, learned to interrupt it by recognizing guilt as information rather than instruction.

"I used to think guilt meant I was doing something wrong," she said. "Now I understand that guilt often means I'm doing something different. When I feel guilty about setting a boundary, I pause and ask, Am I actually harming someone, or am I just violating an old pattern?"

This shift from guilt-as-truth to guilt-as-information allowed Rachel to make conscious choices rather than automatic accommodations.

The Selfish Myth

Perhaps the most pervasive source of guilt around boundary-setting is the myth that any form of self-prioritization is inherently selfish. This myth creates a false binary: you're either completely selfless (good) or somewhat self-focused (bad).

But this binary ignores the reality that sustainable kindness requires self-care. When you consistently neglect your own needs, you eventually become depleted, resentful, and less capable of genuine generosity.

The Oxygen Mask Principle Airlines instruct passengers to put on their own oxygen masks before helping others not because they want to encourage selfishness, but because you can't help anyone if you're unconscious. The same principle applies to emotional and relational health.

David, a father of three, experienced a breakthrough when he applied this principle to his family life.

"I realized that my constant exhaustion and resentment weren't serving my family," he said. "I thought I was being a good father by saying yes to every request and handling every problem. But my kids were learning that adults don't have needs, that love means self-sacrifice, and that asking for help is selfish."

When David started modeling healthy boundaries and self-care, his children began developing better relationship skills themselves.

"They learned that people can love each other and still have limits," he said.

Guilt vs. Compassion

One of the most powerful shifts in releasing guilt is learning to distinguish between guilt-driven helping and compassion-driven helping.

Guilt-driven helping feels heavy, obligatory, and depleting. It's motivated by fear of judgment, need for approval, or desire to avoid the discomfort of guilt. The focus is on relieving your own emotional discomfort rather than genuinely serving others.

Compassion-driven helping feels light, chosen, and energizing. It's motivated by genuine care and flows from a place of abundance rather than fear. The focus is on understanding and meeting real needs in sustainable ways.

The Energy Test Maria learned to use what she called "the energy test" to distinguish between these two types of helping.

"When someone asks for help, I pay attention to how my body responds," she explained. "If I feel energized and genuinely curious about how I can assist, that's usually compassion. If I feel heavy, pressured, or resentful, that's usually guilt. Both might lead to helping, but the quality and sustainability are completely different."

This simple check helped Maria make more conscious choices about when and how to offer assistance.

Releasing Guilt Practically

Letting go of guilt isn't a one-time decision but an ongoing practice. Here are some approaches that have helped others move from guilt-driven to choice-driven behavior:

Challenge the Guilt Messages When guilt arises about setting boundaries, examine the specific messages it's sending. Ask yourself:

- Is this guilt based on actual harm I'm causing or imagined consequences?
- What would I tell a friend who was in this exact situation?
- Am I responsible for solving this problem, or am I taking on responsibility that isn't mine?
- What's the worst realistic outcome if I maintain my boundary?

Reframe Self-Care as Service Instead of seeing boundary-setting as selfish, try viewing it as a service to others. When you take care of yourself, you're more present, patient, and genuinely helpful in your relationships.

Practice Graduated Exposure Start with small boundaries in low-stakes situations to build your tolerance for guilt. Each time you set a boundary and survive the guilt, you build evidence that self-care doesn't make you a bad person.

Seek Reality Checks Talk to trusted friends or family members about your guilt. Often, others can see clearly that your boundaries are reasonable and healthy, even when guilt makes them feel selfish to you.

The Guilt About Changing

Sometimes the deepest guilt comes not from individual boundary-setting incidents, but from the larger process of changing your patterns altogether. You might feel guilty about "disappointing" people who've grown accustomed to your endless availability, or about "abandoning" family members who've relied on your constant caretaking.

Jennifer's Transformation Guilt Jennifer, the teacher we met in earlier chapters, experienced intense guilt as she reduced her chronic overgiving.

"I felt like I was letting everyone down," she said. "My family started commenting that I seemed 'different,' colleagues noticed I wasn't volunteering for every committee, friends had to make other arrangements when I wasn't immediately available. I felt guilty for changing the person they'd all learned to depend on."

But Jennifer gradually realized that her guilt was about violating others' expectations rather than causing actual harm. "People adjusted," she said. "My family learned to be more self-sufficient, my colleagues stepped up to share responsibilities, my friends developed more reciprocal relationships with me. The 'disappointment' I was so worried about causing was actually growth I was facilitating."

When Others Use Guilt

As you begin setting boundaries, you might encounter people who try to manipulate you back into overgiving through guilt tactics. They might make comments about how you've "changed," question your priorities, or express hurt that you're no longer constantly available.

These responses usually aren't malicious. They're often attempts to restore familiar dynamics that served the other person's needs. But recognizing them as manipulation attempts rather than valid moral criticisms helps you maintain your boundaries without getting pulled back into old patterns.

Standing Firm with Compassion You can acknowledge others' disappointment without taking responsibility for managing their emotions about your changes.

"I understand this feels different, and I know change can be challenging. I care about you and I'm still here to support you in ways that work for both of us."

This response validates their feelings without accepting guilt for having boundaries.

The Freedom on the Other Side

As you practice releasing guilt and maintaining boundaries, something remarkable happens: you discover that most of your catastrophic fears about self-care don't materialize. People adapt, relationships adjust, and often the changes improve connections by making them more balanced and authentic.

Elena, the nurse practitioner, found that setting boundaries at work actually improved her patient care. "When I stopped covering every shift and working excessive hours, I had more energy and presence for the patients I did see," she said. "The guilt told me I was being selfish, but the reality was that self-care made me a better healthcare provider."

The guilt that feels so morally urgent in the moment often proves to be based on fears rather than facts. Learning to sit with the discomfort of guilt while maintaining healthy boundaries teaches you that you can tolerate difficult emotions without automatically accommodating others to make them go away.

Guilt as Information, Not Instruction

The goal isn't to never feel guilt again. Guilt can provide valuable information about your values and relationships. But learning to treat guilt as information rather than instruction allows you to make conscious choices rather than automatic accommodations.

When guilt arises, instead of immediately changing your behavior to relieve it, try asking, What is this guilt telling me about my fears, my values, or my patterns? Is this guilt based on current reality or old programming? What would I choose if I weren't afraid?

This curiosity about guilt rather than obedience to it creates space for conscious choice. You might still choose to help or accommodate sometimes, but it becomes a decision made from clarity rather than a compulsion driven by emotional discomfort.

Releasing guilt is one of the most liberating aspects of transforming overgiving patterns. When you're no longer driven by guilt about normal human needs for boundaries, rest, and reciprocity, you can begin building relationships based on mutual respect rather than one-sided accommodation.

In the next chapter, we'll explore how to establish boundaries that feel authentic and sustainable. Boundaries that serve both your well-being and your relationships. Because the goal isn't to become selfish or uncaring, but to create a framework for genuine, sustainable kindness.

CHAPTER 8

ESTABLISH BOUNDARIES

The first boundary I ever set consciously was laughably small: I told my roommate I wouldn't wash her dishes anymore. After months of coming home to a sink full of her dirty plates and automatically cleaning them to avoid conflict, I finally said, "I'm happy to clean up after myself, but I won't be washing your dishes going forward."

Her response? "Oh, okay. I didn't realize that bothered you."

That was it. No drama, no anger, no relationship catastrophe. Just acknowledgment and adjustment. I'd spent months building up resentment and washing dishes I didn't want to wash, imagining that setting this boundary would create massive conflict. The reality was so much simpler than my anxiety had predicted.

That tiny boundary taught me something profound: most of my fears about boundary-setting were bigger than the actual consequences. I'd been avoiding boundaries not because they were dangerous, but because I'd never learned how to set them in ways that felt kind, clear, and sustainable.

From Pattern Recognition to Boundary Setting

Understanding your patterns and examining your beliefs is crucial foundational work, but it's the boundary-setting that transforms your daily reality. The people we've followed through their journeys of recognition and insight were about to discover that implementing boundaries required a different set of skills altogether.

Jenna's Sister Boundary Jenna, the marketing director who'd discovered her anxiety-rescue pattern with her sister, knew that understanding her pattern wasn't enough. Every time her sister called with a crisis, Jenna still felt that familiar surge of anxiety and the compulsion to immediately offer solutions, time, and resources.

"I could see what I was doing," Jenna said, "but I still felt powerless to stop it. My sister would sound overwhelmed, and my whole nervous system would activate like it was my emergency to solve."

Jenna's breakthrough came when she realized that boundaries weren't walls to keep her sister out – they were frameworks that could allow her to care without drowning. Her first attempt at setting a boundary happened during one of her sister's characteristic crisis calls about work stress.

Instead of immediately offering to research solutions, schedule meetings with her sister's boss, or take over project management tasks, Jenna tried something different: "That sounds really stressful. I believe you can handle this, and I'm not the right person to solve work problems that aren't mine. I love you and I'm here to listen if you want to talk through your own ideas."

Her sister's response surprised her: "Oh. I guess I was hoping you'd fix it for me like you usually do. But you're right – it's my job, not yours."

That conversation taught Jenna that her rescue pattern hadn't just been driven by her own anxiety – it had also been enabled by her sister's learned dependence on Jenna's problem-solving. The boundary served both of them by requiring her sister to develop her own capacity while protecting Jenna from taking responsibility for problems that weren't hers.

Learning What Boundaries Actually Are

David, the engineer who'd discovered his automatic problem-solving pattern, had to learn that healthy boundaries weren't about becoming unhelpful or uncaring. They were about creating sustainable ways to show up for people.

After recognizing how his immediate solution-offering prevented others from processing their own feelings and developing their own capabilities, David knew he needed to change his response pattern. But his first attempts at boundaries felt harsh and rejecting.

When his teenage daughter complained about friend drama, David's old pattern would have been to outline communication strategies and conflict resolution techniques. His first boundary attempt swung too far in the opposite direction: "That's your problem to figure out."

His daughter's hurt response – "I wasn't asking you to solve it, Dad. I just wanted you to care" – helped David understand that boundaries weren't about becoming unavailable. They were about being available in more helpful ways.

David learned to pause and ask, "Do you want me to listen, or do you want suggestions?" This simple question allowed him to be present for his daughter without automatically jumping into fix-it mode. When she wanted suggestions, he could offer them consciously rather than compulsively.

"I realized that being helpful and being overwhelming aren't the same thing," David said. "My daughter actually appreciated my input more when she specifically asked for it rather than having it automatically imposed on every conversation."

The Elements That Make Boundaries Work

Jennifer, the teacher who'd tracked her pattern evolution over six months, discovered that effective boundaries needed three essential qualities: they had to be clear, kind, and consistent.

Clarity Through Trial and Error Jennifer's first attempts at boundaries were vague and ineffective. When colleagues began asking her to cover classes, organize events, and take on extra responsibilities beyond her job description, Jennifer's initial boundary was unclear: "I need to focus more on my own work."

This led to confusion and continued requests because colleagues didn't understand what Jennifer was and wasn't available for. She learned to be much more specific: "I'm not available to cover classes outside my normal schedule, but I'm happy to help brainstorm coverage solutions when needed."

Kindness Without Accommodation Jennifer initially thought that boundaries required her to be cold or rejecting. When a colleague asked her to organize the staff holiday party for the third year in a row, Jennifer's first boundary attempt felt harsh: "Find someone else. I'm done being the party planner."

She realized she could be firm about her limits while still being respectful: "I've organized the party for the past two years, and I need to pass that responsibility to someone else this time. I'm happy to share my notes and contacts with whoever takes it on."

This approach honored the relationship while maintaining the boundary. Her colleagues felt supported rather than rejected, even though Jennifer was declining to take on the responsibility.

Consistency Despite Discomfort The most challenging aspect for Jennifer was maintaining boundaries when they felt uncomfortable in the moment. When the principal asked her to chair yet another committee, Jennifer felt enormous pressure to say yes because she'd always been the reliable volunteer.

"I wanted to maintain my boundary, but I also didn't want to disappoint him or seem uncooperative," she said. "I had to learn that temporary discomfort from saying no was better than long-term resentment from saying yes."

Jennifer's consistent boundary-setting gradually changed how colleagues and administrators viewed her availability. Instead of being seen as the person who would automatically take on extra work, she became known as someone who was selective about her commitments and therefore more reliable for the things she did agree to do.

When Boundaries Feel Mean

Rebecca, the lawyer who'd discovered her belief that "love is conditional on performance," struggled intensely with the fear that setting boundaries would make her selfish or mean.

Her turning point came with her elderly parents, who had developed a pattern of calling her multiple times a week with various requests for help, research, and emotional support. Rebecca had been dropping everything to respond to these calls, often working late into the evening to catch up on her own responsibilities.

Rebecca's first boundary attempt felt cruel to her: "I can't be available for every crisis. You need to figure some things out for yourselves."

But she realized she'd created a false choice between being endlessly available and being rejecting. She tried a different approach that honored both her care for her parents and her own capacity: "I love you both and I want to support you. I've been feeling overwhelmed trying to respond to every call immediately. Can we schedule a weekly time to really talk and address any issues that have come up, and save the spontaneous calls for genuine emergencies?"

This boundary allowed Rebecca to be present for her parents in a more intentional way while protecting her from the constant interruptions that had been fragmenting her workdays and evenings.

Her parents initially resisted the change, but over time they appreciated having more meaningful conversations with Rebecca rather than using her as an on-demand research and emotional support service.

"I realized that my endless availability wasn't actually serving them well either," Rebecca said. "It was enabling them to avoid developing their own problem-solving skills and preventing us from having real conversations instead of just crisis management calls."

Dealing with Pushback

Not everyone gracefully accepted the boundaries that Jenna, David, Jennifer, and Rebecca began setting. Learning to maintain boundaries under pressure became an essential skill for all of them.

Jenna's Family Resistance When Jenna stopped automatically rescuing her sister from every crisis, other family members noticed and commented. Her mother called to express concern: "Your sister says you're not helping her anymore. She's really struggling, and it's not like you to be so unsupportive."

Jenna's first impulse was to apologize and return to her old rescuing pattern. But she'd learned to recognize pushback as information about family dynamics rather than evidence that her boundary was wrong.

"I realized that my family had gotten used to me being the problem-solver for everyone," Jenna said. "My boundary forced them to look at how we'd all been participating in a dynamic where my sister never had to develop her own coping skills because I was always there to fix things."

Jenna responded to her mother with what she called "loving firmness": "I care about her deeply, and I'm not helping her by solving problems that she's capable of handling herself. I'm still here to listen and support her, but I won't be managing her life anymore."

Over time, Jenna's sister began developing more confidence in her own problem-solving abilities, and their relationship became more balanced and less crisis-driven.

Different Relationships, Different Approaches

Each person discovered that boundary-setting required different approaches depending on the relationship context, but the core principles remained consistent.

David's Workplace Boundaries David found that professional boundaries needed to be more subtle than family boundaries. When colleagues and clients began expecting immediate solutions to every problem they presented, David couldn't directly say "That's not my job to solve."

Instead, he learned to redirect conversations: "That's an interesting challenge. What approaches have you considered?" or "What do you think might work in this situation?" This allowed him to be helpful without automatically taking ownership of others' problems.

David also established time boundaries around his availability for consultation. Rather than being constantly interruptible, he designated specific times for colleague questions and stuck to them consistently.

"I became more valuable to my team because my input was more intentional," David said. "When people knew they had limited access to my problem-solving, they came more prepared and thought through issues more thoroughly before asking for help."

Jennifer's Professional Evolution Jennifer's boundary work at school required balancing her desire to be a dedicated teacher with her need to maintain sustainable work practices.

When asked to take on responsibilities beyond her job description, Jennifer learned to pause and evaluate whether the request aligned with her professional goals and current capacity. She could say yes to opportunities that genuinely excited her while declining those that felt obligatory.

"I went from being the teacher who said yes to everything to being the teacher who was selective about her commitments," she said. "Ironically, this made me more effective because I could put real energy into the things I chose to take on."

The Compound Effect of Boundaries

As each person developed their boundary-setting skills, they noticed that the benefits extended far beyond the specific situations where they'd implemented limits.

Rebecca discovered that setting boundaries with her parents gave her more energy and presence for her legal work and other relationships. Jenna found that stepping back from her sister's crises allowed her to be more supportive when genuine emergencies arose. David's family appreciated his input more when it came from genuine engagement rather than automatic problem-solving mode.

Jennifer summed up the transformation: "I thought boundaries would make me less caring, but they actually made me more caring. When I'm not constantly overextended, I can show up fully for the commitments I do make. People get the best of me instead of the exhausted, resentful version that comes from always saying yes."

The Ongoing Practice

All four people learned that boundary-setting isn't a one-time skill you master, but an ongoing practice that evolves as relationships and circumstances change.

Jenna discovered that her boundaries with her sister needed periodic adjustment as both of their lives changed. David found that different projects and team dynamics required different approaches to his availability. Jennifer learned to anticipate times of year when boundary pressures would be higher and prepare accordingly. Rebecca realized that her parents' changing needs would require ongoing boundary negotiations.

The goal of boundary-setting isn't to become rigid or unavailable. It's to create frameworks for sustainable relationships where you can be genuinely present and helpful within limits that protect your wellbeing and effectiveness.

Boundaries aren't walls that keep people out – they're the foundation that allows authentic relationships to flourish. When people know what you can and can't do, they stop asking for things you can't provide and start appreciating what you can offer.

In the next chapter, we'll explore how these boundary skills support the larger project of aligning your external behavior with your authentic values and identity – living as who you really are beneath all the accommodating and people-pleasing.

CHAPTER 9

ALIGN WITH THE REAL YOU

Six months after I started setting boundaries and changing my overgiving patterns, a friend made an observation that stopped me in my tracks: "You seem more like yourself lately. I can't quite put my finger on it, but you feel more... authentic."

I knew exactly what she meant, though I couldn't have articulated it at the time. For years, I'd been living as a carefully curated version of myself – the helpful one, the accommodating one, the one who never caused problems or created inconvenience. But as I'd gradually stopped performing that character, something unexpected had emerged: the person I actually was underneath all that people-pleasing.

The journey from recognizing patterns to examining beliefs to setting boundaries had been preparation for this deeper work: learning to align my external life with my internal truth. It wasn't enough to stop overgiving – I needed to discover what authentic giving looked like. It wasn't sufficient to set boundaries – I had to figure out what I actually wanted to protect and nurture within those boundaries.

This chapter is about that alignment process: how to move from performing kindness to embodying it, from accommodating others to honoring yourself, from living by others' expectations to following your own values.

Rediscovering Your Authentic Self

After years of accommodation and people-pleasing, many people discover they've lost touch with who they are beneath all the performed agreeableness. The process of rediscovering your authentic self can feel both exhilarating and terrifying.

When Jennifer stopped automatically volunteering for every committee and covering every extra shift, she experienced an unexpected identity crisis. "I'd organized my entire identity around being useful," she said. "When I stopped constantly helping others, I had all this time and energy I didn't know what to do with. I felt lost."

This disorientation is common and temporary. Your authentic self hasn't disappeared – it's been buried under layers of accommodation and performance. The excavation process begins with small experiments in preference and choice.

Start by paying attention to what you actually enjoy rather than what you think you should enjoy. Notice which activities energize you and which drain you. Observe your natural rhythms and preferences without immediately judging them as selfish or impractical.

Jennifer began this process by simply noticing her authentic responses throughout the day. She discovered she preferred small gatherings to large parties, that she loved gardening but had been too busy to pursue it, that certain types of teaching challenges energized her while others depleted her.

"It was like getting to know myself for the first time," she said. "I realized I'd been so focused on being what others needed that I'd never asked what I needed or wanted."

The process isn't always comfortable. You might feel selfish for having preferences or guilty for enjoying activities that don't directly benefit others. This discomfort is part of the alignment process – you're learning to tolerate being yourself instead of being what others need.

Distinguishing Values from Obligations

One of the most profound shifts in alignment work is learning to distinguish between actions that flow from your authentic values and actions that stem from obligation, guilt, or fear.

Rebecca had to learn the difference between genuinely wanting to help her parents and feeling obligated to manage their lives. Her breakthrough came when she asked herself: "If I knew my parents would love me regardless of how much I helped them, what would I choose to do?"

The answer surprised her. Without the pressure of earning love through service, Rebecca realized she genuinely enjoyed weekly conversations with her parents and helping them navigate complex decisions. But she had no authentic desire to drop everything for non-urgent requests or solve problems they were capable of handling themselves.

This distinction between values-based and obligation-based helping is crucial for authentic alignment. Values-based actions feel energizing and sustainable even when they're challenging. Obligation-based actions feel heavy and depleting even when they're easy.

To identify the difference in your own life, pay attention to your internal experience when making choices. Actions that align with your values typically feel like "I want to" or "This matters to me." Actions that stem from obligation feel like "I have to" or "I should."

This doesn't mean you'll never do things you don't enjoy – sometimes authentic values include commitments that require discipline or sacrifice. But even these challenging choices feel different when they come from genuine choice rather than external pressure.

Honoring Your Natural Rhythms and Preferences

Part of authentic alignment involves recognizing and honoring your natural rhythms, energy patterns, and ways of being in the world. Many chronic overgivers have spent so long adapting to others' needs that they've lost touch with their own natural pace and preferences.

David discovered that he had natural rhythms his overgiving had been violating for years. "I'm naturally someone who processes things slowly and deliberately," he said. "But when people came to me with problems, I felt pressure to have immediate solutions. I was performing quick responsiveness instead of honoring my natural reflective approach."

Understanding your authentic way of being in the world requires honest self-assessment without immediate judgment about whether your natural tendencies are "good" or "bad." Some people are naturally quick decision-makers; others need time to process. Some are energized by social interaction; others need solitude to recharge. Some work best with detailed plans; others thrive with flexibility.

When David began working according to his authentic rhythms rather than others' expectations, the results surprised everyone. His responses became more thoughtful and effective because they came from genuine reflection rather than pressured quick-thinking.

The key is distinguishing between accommodating others' preferences and violating your own nature. Flexibility and consideration are valuable qualities, but not when they require you to consistently act against your authentic way of being.

Moving from Performed to Authentic Generosity

As you learn to align with your authentic self, you'll discover that genuine generosity feels completely different from performed kindness. Authentic giving is energizing rather than depleting, sustainable rather than exhausting, and truly beneficial rather than enabling.

When Jenna stopped automatically rescuing her sister from every crisis, she worried she was becoming selfish and uncaring. But when her sister faced a genuine health crisis requiring surgery and recovery support, Jenna's response came from authentic care rather than anxiety-driven compulsion.

"I felt clear about what I could and wanted to offer," Jenna said. "I offered specific support that matched both her needs and my capacity. It felt generous rather than obligatory."

The difference between authentic and performed generosity becomes clear when you pay attention to your internal experience:

Authentic generosity feels chosen, energizing, and sustainable. You're clear about what you can offer and comfortable with your limits. Your help addresses real needs without creating dependency.

Performed generosity feels obligatory, depleting, and unsustainable. You're unclear about your limits and uncomfortable saying no. Your help often enables rather than empowers the recipient.

This shift from performed to authentic generosity often means giving less frequently but more meaningfully. Quality replaces quantity, and genuine care replaces anxious accommodation.

Developing Internal Standards

Authentic alignment requires developing internal standards for your life rather than constantly adapting to external expectations. This means getting clear about what matters to you, what you value, and what kind of person you want to be – independent of others' opinions or approval.

Years of people-pleasing had left Jennifer with what she called "a committee of everyone else's voices" guiding her decisions. She'd internalized so many different people's standards and expectations that she had no idea what she actually believed about how to live.

Developing internal standards begins with identifying your core values – not what you think you should value, but what genuinely matters to you. These values become the framework for making decisions when external pressures conflict with internal truth.

Jennifer decided that she valued depth over breadth in relationships, meaning over busyness in work, and intentionality over automatic responsiveness in daily choices. These weren't revolutionary principles, but they were authentically hers.

"Having my own standards gave me a framework for making decisions," she said. "Instead of asking 'What will make others happy?' I could ask 'What aligns with what I actually value?'"

Your internal standards don't need to be complex or profound. They just need to be genuinely yours and consistently applied to your choices and relationships.

Tolerating the Discomfort of Authenticity

Living authentically often involves tolerating discomfort that accommodation has been helping you avoid. When you stop automatically agreeing, accommodating, and overgiving, you encounter situations that require navigating conflict, disappointment, and uncertainty.

Rebecca found that being authentic in relationships created anxiety she'd been avoiding through performance patterns. "When I stopped automatically agreeing with everyone, I had to deal with disagreement," she said. "When I stopped managing everyone's emotions, I had to tolerate others being upset."

This discomfort is temporary and necessary. All your accommodating has been a way of controlling outcomes – ensuring that people stay happy with you by being agreeable enough, helpful enough, available enough. Authenticity means giving up that illusion of control.

The fears that drive accommodation – rejection, conflict, disapproval – usually turn out to be less dangerous than anticipated. Most people respect authenticity more than performance, even when your authentic response isn't what they hoped for.

Learning to tolerate the discomfort of being yourself, rather than managing others' comfort through self-sacrifice, is essential for sustainable authenticity.

Navigating Relationship Changes

As you become more authentic, your relationships will change. Some will deepen and improve as people gain access to the real you. Others may become strained or fade away as dynamics shift. All of them will become more honest.

David discovered that his shift toward authenticity acted like a filter on relationships. People who valued him for his genuine self appreciated the changes. People who'd primarily valued his automatic helpfulness were less comfortable with the new dynamic.

"Some colleagues started coming to me less frequently because they knew I wouldn't just give them immediate solutions," David said. "But the ones who stayed appreciated the quality of interaction more. My relationships became fewer but deeper."

This relationship evolution is natural and healthy. Relationships based on your performance were never fully authentic anyway – they were connections to a version of you rather than to you yourself.

The people who truly care about you will adjust to your increased authenticity, even if they need time to adapt to the changes. The people who can't accept your authentic self were primarily invested in what you could do for them rather than who you are.

Daily Alignment Practice

Alignment isn't a destination but an ongoing practice of checking in with yourself and adjusting your external life to match your internal truth.

Jenna developed regular "authenticity check-ins" – moments throughout the day when she'd pause and ask whether her choices were coming from genuine desire or automatic pattern. "Before agreeing to something, I started asking myself: Am I saying yes because I want to, or because I think I should?"

These simple check-ins help catch yourself before falling back into old patterns of automatic accommodation. They also help you notice when you're making choices from fear rather than authenticity.

Other helpful alignment practices include regular reflection on whether your current commitments match your values, periodic assessment of your energy levels and satisfaction, and conscious choice-making rather than automatic responsiveness to requests and opportunities.

The Ripple Effect of Authentic Living

As you become more aligned with your authentic self, the changes affect every area of life, not just your overgiving patterns. Authenticity in relationships creates permission for authenticity in work, creativity, and personal choices.

Jennifer found that being genuine in relationships gave her courage to pursue creative projects she'd always deemed "impractical." Rebecca discovered that authenticity was energizing in ways performance never was. David found that his authentic approach created permission for others to be genuine too.

The goal of alignment work isn't to become selfish or uncaring. It's to become genuinely caring in sustainable ways that honor both yourself and others. When you know who you are and what you value, you can give from abundance rather than depletion, serve from choice rather than compulsion, and love from freedom rather than fear.

This personal transformation creates the foundation for a new kind of kindness – one that serves both giver and receiver, builds rather than depletes, and creates genuine connection rather than functional dependency. In our final chapter, we'll explore how this authentic alignment enables truly sustainable and beneficial generosity.

CHAPTER 10

EMBODY A NEW KINDNESS

The most surprising thing about learning to stop overgiving wasn't how much energy I gained or how much resentment disappeared. It was how much kinder I became.

This revelation came slowly, then all at once. Friends began commenting that I seemed more present when I helped them. Family members said my support felt more genuine and substantial. Colleagues noted that my input carried more weight because they knew it came from careful consideration rather than automatic agreement.

I was giving less frequently but more meaningfully. My kindness had transformed from an anxious performance into an authentic expression of care. Instead of helping from fear, obligation, or guilt, I was helping from choice, wisdom, and genuine affection.

This is the paradox of recovering from detrimental kindness: you don't become less caring – you become more effectively caring. You don't lose your generous nature – you learn to express it sustainably. You don't abandon kindness – you embody a new kind of kindness that serves everyone better.

This final chapter is about that new kindness: what it looks like, how it feels, and how to cultivate it as your overgiving patterns continue to evolve and heal.

The Characteristics of Conscious Kindness

The kindness that emerges from authentic alignment has distinct qualities that set it apart from both detrimental overgiving and selfish withholding. Understanding these characteristics helps you recognize and cultivate this new way of caring.

It's Chosen, Not Compulsive Conscious kindness flows from deliberate choice rather than automatic response. When someone needs help, you pause and assess: Do I have capacity? Is this genuinely helpful? Does this align with my values and the relationship's dynamics?

Jennifer discovered this difference when a colleague asked her to take on extra responsibilities during a busy period. Instead of automatically saying yes, she took time to consider whether the request made sense. "I realized I could offer specific support that matched both her needs and my capacity without taking over her entire project," she said.

This pause between request and response transforms kindness from reactive accommodation into conscious generosity. You're helping because you choose to, not because you feel you have to.

It's Sustainable, Not Depleting Conscious kindness operates within your genuine capacity rather than stretching you beyond sustainable limits. It recognizes that depleting yourself in service of others ultimately serves no one well.

David learned to offer help in ways that energized rather than exhausted him. "I started paying attention to what kinds of support I could give from my natural strengths versus what required me to perform beyond my capacity," he said. "When I helped from my authentic abilities, it felt good for both of us."

This sustainability isn't about being selfish – it's about being realistic. Sustainable kindness can continue over time because it doesn't require constant self-sacrifice or boundary violations.

It's Empowering, Not Enabling Conscious kindness considers the long-term impact of help rather than just providing immediate relief. It asks whether your assistance will build the other person's capacity or create dependency.

When Jenna's sister faced genuine challenges, Jenna learned to offer support that strengthened rather than weakened her sister's confidence. "Instead of solving her problems, I started asking questions that helped her think through solutions herself," Jenna said. "I realized that my 'help' was often preventing her from developing her own capabilities."

This shift from rescuing to empowering requires trusting others' ability to handle their own lives while offering appropriate support when genuinely needed.

It's Honest, Not Performed Conscious kindness includes the ability to be truthful about what you can and can't offer, what you're comfortable with and what crosses your boundaries. It doesn't require you to pretend enthusiasm you don't feel or capacity you don't have.

Rebecca learned to help her parents in ways that felt genuine rather than obligatory. "I stopped pretending I was available for every crisis and started being honest about when I could genuinely be present," she said. "Paradoxically, this made my support more valuable because they knew it was real."

This honesty creates deeper trust in relationships because people know they're getting your authentic response rather than a performance designed to please them.

The Energy of Authentic Generosity

One of the most noticeable differences between conscious kindness and overgiving is the quality of energy involved. Conscious kindness feels light, flowing, and sustainable, while overgiving feels heavy, forced, and depleting.

Recognition Through Energy Learning to recognize the energy signature of different types of helping becomes a valuable compass for navigating generosity. When considering whether to help someone, pay attention to how the possibility feels in your body.

Does thinking about helping feel expansive or constrictive? Energizing or draining? Open or pressured? These physical sensations provide information about whether your potential help comes from authentic generosity or compulsive accommodation.

Jenna learned to use what she called "the lightness test": "If thinking about helping someone feels heavy and obligatory, I know it's coming from my old rescue pattern. If it feels light and clear, it's probably genuine care."

The Flow State of Giving Conscious kindness often feels effortless, even when it requires significant time or energy. This isn't because the help itself is easy, but because it flows from your authentic nature rather than fighting against it.

David noticed this when he began helping colleagues in ways that matched his natural problem-solving style rather than forcing immediate responses. "When I helped from my authentic strengths and at my natural pace, even complex assistance felt flowing rather than forced," he said.

This flow state indicates alignment between your giving and your genuine capacity, values, and way of being in the world.

Boundaries as Acts of Kindness

One of the most profound shifts in understanding kindness is recognizing that boundaries themselves are acts of care – both for yourself and others. Clear limits create safety, trust, and sustainability in relationships.

Kindness to Others Through Boundaries When you maintain clear boundaries, you help others know how to be in relationship with you successfully. You prevent them from unknowingly crossing lines that would damage the relationship. You model healthy self-care that gives them permission to have their own limits.

Jennifer discovered that her workplace boundaries actually improved her relationships with colleagues. "When people knew what I was and wasn't available for, they stopped making requests I'd have to decline. Our interactions became more efficient and less awkward."

Clear boundaries also prevent the resentment that builds when you consistently accommodate beyond your capacity. By protecting yourself from overextension, you protect the relationship from the tension that comes with hidden resentment.

Kindness to Yourself Through Limits Boundaries are also acts of self-compassion that honor your needs, capacity, and wellbeing. They recognize that your welfare matters and deserves protection.

Rebecca learned to see boundary-setting as self-care rather than selfishness. "I realized that taking care of myself wasn't separate from taking care of others – it was the foundation that made caring for others possible," she said.

This self-kindness creates the internal resources necessary for genuine generosity. When you're well-cared for, you can offer care from abundance rather than depletion.

The Art of Saying No Kindly

Conscious kindness includes the ability to decline requests gracefully and warmly. Saying no doesn't require you to be harsh, apologetic, or elaborate in your explanations.

Clear and Warm Declinations The goal is to be both definitive and kind in your response. This means saying no clearly enough that the person understands your position, while maintaining warmth that honors the relationship.

Instead of: "I'm so sorry, I wish I could help but I'm just completely overwhelmed right now and I feel terrible about it but I just can't take on anything else."

Try: "I care about you and I'm not available to help with this. I hope you find good support for the project."

This approach respects both your limits and the other person's need for a clear response. It doesn't leave room for negotiation while maintaining relational warmth.

No Apology Required Conscious kindness recognizes that you don't need to apologize for having limits or for declining requests that don't align with your capacity or values. Apologizing for reasonable boundaries suggests that having limits is somehow wrong.

David learned to decline requests matter-of-factly: "That doesn't work for me, but I hope you find someone who can help." This straightforward approach felt more honest and respectful than elaborate apologies that implied his boundaries were problematic.

Helping from Strength, Not Weakness

Conscious kindness flows from your genuine strengths and resources rather than from fear, guilt, or the need to prove your worth. This strength-based helping is more effective and sustainable for everyone involved.

Identifying Your Gifts Part of conscious kindness involves understanding what you authentically have to offer and what feels forced or unnatural. Your most valuable help usually comes from your natural abilities and genuine interests rather than from attempts to be everything to everyone.

Jennifer discovered that her real gift was creating supportive environments where others could process their own thoughts and feelings. "I stopped trying to give advice about things I didn't understand and started offering the kind of presence and listening that came naturally to me," she said.

This shift from generic helpfulness to specific gifts made Jennifer's support more valuable and less exhausting for her to provide.

Offering What You Have, Not What You Think You Should Have Conscious kindness means offering your actual resources rather than resources you think you should have. If you have time but not money, you offer time. If you have listening capacity but not problem-solving energy, you offer presence.

Rebecca learned to help her parents in ways that matched her actual capacity rather than trying to meet every type of need. "I realized I could offer emotional support and research assistance, but I wasn't good at hands-on caregiving. Instead of feeling guilty about my limitations, I focused on what I could genuinely provide."

The Ripple Effects of Conscious Kindness

When you embody conscious kindness, the effects extend far beyond your immediate relationships. Your modeling of sustainable generosity influences others and contributes to healthier relationship dynamics in your communities.

Permission for Others When you demonstrate that it's possible to be both caring and boundaried, you give others permission to find their own balance between generosity and self-care. Your conscious kindness becomes a model for sustainable relationships.

David noticed that his family members began setting their own boundaries after watching him do so successfully. "My children started saying no to things they didn't want to do, and my spouse began asking for help instead of just accommodating everything. My boundaries gave them permission to have their own."

Breaking Generational Patterns Conscious kindness often interrupts family patterns of overgiving, martyrdom, or unhealthy caretaking that have been passed down through generations. By finding a healthier way to care, you create new possibilities for family relationships.

Jennifer realized that her shift away from chronic overcommitment was teaching her young nieces a different model of adult responsibility. "They're seeing that adults can be helpful and caring without being constantly overwhelmed and resentful," she said.

Creating Healthier Relationship Norms As more people embody conscious kindness, it becomes easier for everyone to maintain sustainable generosity. Communities and families develop healthier expectations about help, reciprocity, and individual responsibility.

The Ongoing Practice

Embodying conscious kindness isn't a destination but an ongoing practice that evolves as you grow and as your relationships change. The goal isn't perfection but rather continuous alignment between your caring impulses and your authentic capacity.

Regular Check-ins Maintaining conscious kindness requires periodic assessment of your patterns, energy levels, and relationship dynamics. Are you slipping back into automatic accommodation? Are your boundaries serving their intended purpose? Is your helping coming from choice or compulsion?

Jenna developed a monthly practice of reviewing her commitments and helping patterns. "I ask myself whether my current giving feels sustainable and authentic, or whether I'm starting to slip back into old patterns," she said.

Flexibility and Adjustment Conscious kindness adapts to changing circumstances while maintaining core principles of sustainability and authenticity. Your boundaries and helping patterns may need adjustment as your life evolves, but the underlying commitment to conscious choice remains constant.

Self-Compassion During Learning Learning to embody conscious kindness is a process that includes mistakes, backsliding, and gradual progress. Treating yourself with compassion during this learning process is essential for sustainable change.

Rebecca found that judging herself harshly when she occasionally fell back into overgiving actually made it harder to return to conscious kindness. "I learned that self-compassion wasn't self-indulgence – it was the foundation for continued growth," she said.

The New Definition of Kindness

Through this journey from detrimental overgiving to conscious kindness, a new definition of caring emerges. Kindness isn't about endless accommodation, self-sacrifice, or automatic yes-saying. It's about thoughtful generosity that serves both giver and receiver sustainably.

True kindness honors the full humanity of everyone involved. It recognizes that both your needs and others' needs matter. It understands that sustainable help is more valuable than unsustainable rescue attempts. It appreciates that authentic care is more meaningful than performed accommodation.

This new kindness creates relationships based on mutual respect rather than functional dependency. It builds individual capacity rather than enabling helplessness. It flows from abundance rather than depletion, from choice rather than compulsion, from love rather than fear.

As you continue embodying this conscious kindness, you'll discover that it's not only more sustainable for you – it's more beneficial for everyone in your life. The people you care about receive more thoughtful, empowering support. Your relationships become more honest and balanced. Your generosity becomes a source of energy rather than exhaustion.

The journey from detrimental kindness to conscious kindness is ultimately a journey home to yourself – to your authentic capacity for care, your genuine values, and your sustainable way of contributing to others' wellbeing. In finding this new kindness, you discover that you haven't lost your caring nature. You've simply learned to express it in ways that honor both your heart and your humanity.

This is the kindness the world needs: thoughtful, sustainable, empowering, and real. It's the kindness you've always been capable of, waiting beneath the performance and overextension. It's the kindness that serves everyone, including you.

ACKNOWLEDGMENTS

This book was born from pain, silence, and eventually liberation.

To the ones who mistook my kindness for weakness, thank you. You helped me wake up.

To my friend Patrick, thank you for being solid. You showed up with real support when I needed it most, and you reminded me why this message matters.

To Kelendria, whose voice still echoes in my heart, you told me I had something worth saying. You believed in this book before it even existed. I carried your encouragement with me through every chapter. This one's for you.

To Geo Derice, thank you for being more than a coach. Your wisdom, accountability, and belief in this message helped me bring it to life. I'm a better man because of you.

To the readers, may this be more than a book. May it be a mirror, a wake-up call, and a watershed moment. May it give you language for what you've felt but couldn't explain and the courage to choose yourself.

There's freedom on the other side of detrimental kindness.

Let's go get it.

ABOUT THE AUTHOR

Jason Johnson is a transformation specialist, speaker, and life coach who helps high-performing professionals, caregivers, and recovering people pleasers stop overgiving and start living with intention. Known for his practical wisdom and compassionate approach, Jason empowers audiences and clients alike to set boundaries, protect their peace, and lead with authenticity without guilt.

With a background in fitness coaching and years spent supporting clients through burnout and emotional fatigue, Jason quickly realized that lasting change requires more than physical transformation. It demands a shift in mindset and self-worth. This insight led him to explore the deeper emotional and psychological roots of overgiving and self-abandonment.

Jason is also the creator of a successful line of mindfulness inspired coloring books. His work bridges the gap between personal development and professional wellness, making him a trusted voice for those ready to reclaim their power and rewrite the rules of kindness.

Whether on stage, in coaching sessions, or through the pages of his books, Jason challenges others to stop shrinking, start healing, and take up space fully and unapologetically.